THE COLLECTED POEMS

ALSO BY Stanley Kunitz

Intellectual Things (poems)

Passport to the War (poems)

Selected Poems 1928–1958

Poems of John Keats (editor)

The Testing-Tree (poems)

Poems of Akhmatova (translator, with Max Hayward)

Story under Full Sail, by Andrei Voznesensky (translator)

The Coat without a Seam (poems: limited edition)

The Terrible Threshold (English edition only)

A Kind of Order, A Kind of Folly: Essays & Conversations

Orchard Lamps, by Ivan Drach (editor and co-translator)

The Poems of Stanley Kunitz 1928–1978

The Wellfleet Whale and Companion Poems (chapbook)

Next-to-Last Things: New Poems and Essays

The Essential Blake (editor)

Interviews and Encounters with Stanley Kunitz

Passing Through: The Later Poems

The Wild Card, Selected Poems of Karl Shapiro
(editor, with David Ignatow)

THE COLLECTED POEMS

Stanley Kunitz

W. W. NORTON & COMPANY

NEW YORK / LONDON

For information about permission to reproduce selections from this book, write to Permissions,
W. W. Norton & Company, Inc., 500 Fifth Avenue, New York, NY 10110

The text and display of this book are composed in Garamond 3
Composition by Matrix Publishing Services
Manufacturing by Haddon Craftsmen Inc.
Book design by BTDync

Library of Congress Cataloging-in-Publication Data
Kunitz, Stanley, date.
{poems}
The collected poems / Stanley Kunitz
p.   cm.
Includes index.
ISBN 0-393-053030-0
PS3521.U7 A17 2000
811'.52—dc21   00-041130
ISBN 0-393-32294-7 pbk.

W. W. Norton & Company, Inc.
500 Fifth Avenue, New York, N.Y. 10110
www.wwnorton.com

W. W. Norton & Company Ltd.
Castle House, 75/76 Wells Street, London W1T 3QT

3 4 5 6 7 8 9 0

CONTENTS

from
PASSPORT TO THE WAR   (1944)

from

THIS GARLAND, DANGER,
in SELECTED POEMS: 1928–1958

from

THE TESTING-TREE   (1971)

from
THE LAYERS,
in THE POEMS OF STANLEY KUNITZ 1928–1978

from
NEXT-TO-LAST THINGS   (1985)

from
PASSING THROUGH: THE LATER POEMS   (1995)

REFLECTIONS

Years ago I came to the realization that the most poignant of all lyric
tensions stems from the awareness that we are living and dying at once.
To embrace such knowledge and yet to remain compassionate and
whole—that is the consummation of the endeavor of art.

At the core of one's existence is a pool of energy that has nothing to do
with personal identity, but that falls away from self, blends into the
natural universe. Man has only a bit part to play in the whole mar-
velous show of creation.

Poems would be easy if our heads weren't so full of the day's clatter.
The task is to get through to the other side, where we can hear the deep
rhythms that connect us with the stars and the tides.

I keep trying to improve my controls over language, so that I won't
have to tell lies. And I keep reading the masters, because they infect me
with human possibility.

Our poems can never satisfy us, since they are at best a diminished echo
of a song that maybe once or twice in a lifetime we've heard and keep
trying to recall.

I like to think that it is the poet's love of particulars, the things of this
world, that leads him to universals.

A badly made thing falls apart. It takes only a few years for most of the
energy to leak out of a defective work of art. To put it simply, conser-
vation of energy is the function of form.

We have all been expelled from the Garden, but the ones who suffer most in exile are those who are still permitted to dream of perfection.

Sometimes I feel ashamed that I've written so few poems on political themes, on the causes that agitate me. But then I remind myself that to choose to live as a poet in the modern superstate is in itself a political action.

There's always a song lying under the surface of my poems. The struggle is between incantation and sense. Incantation wants to take over. It really doesn't need a language: all it needs is sounds. The sense has to struggle to assert itself, to mount the rhythm and become inseparable from it.

In his eighty-seventh year, Miró told an interviewer that he felt closest to "the young—all the young generations." From childhood to age, he ruminated, "I have always lived a very intense life, almost like a monk, an austere life. It comes out in little leaves, floating about, dispersing themselves. But the trunk of the tree and the branches remain solid."

Yes, he admitted, his style had changed—changed several times, in fact, during his long life. But these changes did not imply a rejection of what he had done before.

Looking back, he could see a continuity in the essence of his work, which is nourished at every stage "by all of my past, the great human past. And what looks like a zig-zag is really a straight line."

At my age, after you're done—or ruefully think you're done—with the nagging anxieties and complications of your youth, what is there left for you to confront but the great simplicities? I never tire of bird-song and sky and weather. I want to write poems that are natural, luminous, deep, spare. I dream of an art so transparent that you can look through and see the world.

FROM

INTELLECTUAL THINGS

"For the tear is an intellectual thing."

—WILLIAM BLAKE

1930

CHANGE

Dissolving in the chemic vat
Of time, man (gristle and fat),
Corrupting on a rock in space
That crumbles, lifts his impermanent face
To watch the stars, his brain locked tight
Against the tall revolving night.
Yet is he neither here nor there
Because the mind moves everywhere;
And he is neither now nor then
Because tomorrow comes again
Foreshadowed, and the ragged wing
Of yesterday's remembering
Cuts sharply the immediate moon;
Nor is he always; late and soon
Becoming, never being, till
Becoming is a being still.

Here, Now, and Always, man would be
Inviolate eternally:
This is his spirit's trinity.

SINGLE VISION

Before I am completely shriven
I shall reject my inch of heaven.

Cancel my eyes, and, standing, sink
Into my deepest self; there drink

Memory down. The banner of
My blood, unfurled, will not be love,

Only the pity and the pride
Of it, pinned to my open side.

When I have utterly refined
The composition of my mind,

Shaped language of my marrow till
Its forms are instant to my will,

Suffered the leaf of my heart to fall
Under the wind, and, stripping all

The tender blanket from my bone,
Rise like a skeleton in the sun,

I shall have risen to disown
The good mortality I won.

Directly risen with the stain
Of life upon my crested brain,

Which I shall shake against my ghost
To frighten him, when I am lost.

Gladly, as any poison, yield
My halved conscience, brightly peeled;

Infect him, since we live but once,
With the unused evil in my bones.

I'll shed the tear of souls, the true
Sweat, Blake's intellectual dew,

Before I am resigned to slip
A dusty finger on my lip.

PARTICULAR LULLABY

Declines at evening from your eyes,
Like summer slipping down a tree,
Your noon-high pride: but not your wise,
Your sensitive pleased beauty.

The ebb of spirit from the vase
Of woman is the hurt extreme
Of conscious breath. Bewilder your thighs,
Wrap your long thought in a dream.

By image of all hush, a mist
Of blossom on the feminine bough,
Annul the runner in your wrist,
The small clock throbbing in your brow.

On present time's derisive hope
Then break, O ever of your smile:
Sunbreak of lips, from tropic sleep,
Dazzle the impossible meanwhile.

Promise Me

Only, when I am sudden loss
Of consequence for mind and stair,
Picking my dogged way from us
To whom, recessive in some where
Of recollection, with the cross
Fallen, the breast in disrepair:

Only, when loosening clothes, you lean
Out of your window sleepily,
And with luxurious, lidded mien
Sniff at the bitter dark—dear she,
Think somewhat gently of, between
Love ended and beginning, me.

STRANGE CALENDAR

Considered by the logical brief clock
That keeps no reckoning of blood's unreason,
I cannot board your minute at the dock
Of this perpetual departure; I cannot wake
Beside your name, for having welcomed light in a later season.

Suppose my punctual hat should not arrive
Tonight at that known corner where the eyes
Expect: if you should stand engraved with love
Until through annuals of space I came to wive
Your precarious dear doom—suppose, My Early One, suppose—

Or even should your restless feet have fled,
Yet one of me, arrived, shall pace the square;
And one of me shall watch your not mine bed,
Breathing upon your sleep; another shall have laid
Himself in the revolving rock and, ageless, wait you there.

POEM

O Heart: this is a dream I had, or not a dream.
Lovingly, lovingly, I wept, but my tears did not rhyme.

In the year of my mother's blood, when I was born,
She buried my innocent head in a field, because the earth

Was sleepy with the winter. And I spoke the corn,
And I cried the clover up, with the dewy mouth of my mirth.

In the honey of summer my brain conceived: a child, I flowered
Over the maiden-stalks, drinking sweet upper light,

For I was intimate with the sun, till he devoured
Me utterly, O Heart, his tenderest neophyte.

So I died. Small gluttonous birds picked on my limpid brow,
My pale drooped feet were manacled with rushing worms;

And when I was sufficiently dead (Torturer Thou!)
I was born again. Dissolving, memory reforms

The cyclic hour I pulled life's bony root, slow inch
By inch, from its loamy trap; shrilly, like a mandrake, screamed

To rip the cord, suck liberal air, after the pinch
Of planetary rock. Womanly, a shadow combed

Her dark tremendous hair beyond the violet border
Of my sleep. Strong passionate hands I had, but could not find

The red position of her heart, nor the subtle order
Of her lips and breasts, nor the breathing cities of her mind.

Lovingly, lovingly, I wept for her absent eyes,
Large pity of her thought; I broke the spine of my pride

Upon a stone, seeing she did not recognize
My tears, because our sorrows did not coincide.

Softly grieving, ironic at the gates of horn,
I took my baffled head and buried it under the corn.

O Heart: this is a dream I had, or not a dream.

DECIDUOUS BRANCH

Winter, that coils in the thickets now,
Will glide from the fields; the swinging rain
Be knotted with flowers; on every bough
A bird will meditate again.

Lord, in the night if I should die,
Who entertained your thrilling worm,
Corruption wastes more than the eye
Can pick from this imperfect form.

I lie awake, hearing the drip
Upon my sill; thinking, the sun
Has not been promised; we who strip
Summer to seed shall be undone.

Now, while the antler of the eaves
Liquefies, drop by drop, I brood
On a Christian thing: unless the leaves
Perish, the tree is not renewed.

If all our perishable stuff
Be nourished to its rot, we clean
Our trunk of death, and in our tough
And final growth are evergreen.

THE WORDS OF THE PREACHER

Taking infection from the vulgar air
And sick with the extravagant disease
Of life, my soul rejected the sweet snare
Of happiness; declined
That democratic bait, set in the world
By fortune's old and mediocre mind.

To love a changing shape with perfect faith
Is waste of faith; to follow dying things
With deathless hope is vain; to go from breath
To breath, so to be fed
And put to sleep, is cheat and shame—because
By piecemeal living a man is doomed, I said.

For time with clever fingers ties the knot
Of life that is extended like a rope,
And bundling up the spinning of our thought
(The ribbons and the lace
That might have made a garment for the wind),
Constricts our substance to a cipher's space.

Into the middle of my thought I crept
And on the bosom of the angel lay,
Lived all my life at once; and oh I wept
At what I could foresee;
Upon his death-soft burning plumage wept
To vie with God for His eternity.

AMBERGRIS

This body, tapped of every drop of breath,
In vast corruption of its swollen pride,
Proclaims itself the very whale of death;
Yet, I believe, the hand that plumbs its side
Will gather dissolution's sweet increase.
Exquisite fern of death—in nature, ambergris.

Meanwhile, thinking of love, I have been dressed
For such destruction. Though it surely break,
Come pluck the deep wild kernel of my breast,
That wafer of devotion, and partake
Of its compacted sweetness, till it bring
The soul to rise upon the fleshly wing.

If gentle heart be scorned, in scorn of it
I shall immerse it in such bitterness,
Bathe every pulse in such an acid wit,
That from my mammoth, cold, and featureless
Event of age, my enemies will flee,
Whereas my friends will stay and pillage me.

APPROACH OF AUTUMN

The early violets we saw together,
Lifting their delicate swift heads
As if to dip them in the water, now wither,
Arching no more like thoroughbreds.

Slender and pale, they flee the rime
Of death: the ghosts of violets
Are running in a dream. Heart-flowering time
Decays, green goes, and the eye forgets.

Forgets? But what spring-blooded stock
Sprouts deathless violets in the skull
That, pawing on the hard and bitter rock
Of reason, make thinking beautiful?

THE PIVOT

He heard the centuries tick slowly,
Earth's pulse equivocate. *O Lord,*
Gigantic silence strikes: Thy holy
And undeniable Word.

This is the bitter promised day
When, dragging wings, he leaves behind
A faunlike head upon a tray,
Spear buried in the mind.

Now he must tread the starry wrack
And penetrate the burning sea.
Dearly beloved, I may come back,
But do not wait for me.

HE

He runs before the wise men: he
Is moving on the hills like snow.
No gifts, no tears, no company
He brings, but wind-rise and water-flow.

In meadows of descended day
His motion leans, dividing air:
He takes the unforgiving way
Beneath the apostolic star.

She who has known him calls him stranger.
Parting the night's long hair, he steals
Within the heart, that humble manger
Where the white, astonished spirit kneels.

His vertical inflicting pride,
Whose shadow cuts the nib of space,
Bends to this virtue fructified.
But though he kiss the little face

Like rapture breaking on the mind,
The necessary fierce details
Implacably he has designed.
Redemption hangs upon the nails.

Very Tree

Forget the tube of bark,
Alliterative leaves,
Tenacious like a hand
Gnarled rootage in the dark
Interior of land.

Bright incidental bird
Whose melody is fanned
Among the bundled sheaves,
Wild spool of the winding word,
Reject: and let there be
Only tree.

Earth's absolute arithmetic
Of being is not in the flowering stick
Filled with the sperm of sun,
But in a figure seen
Behind our eyelids when we close
Slow petals of the brain
To match the night's repose.

Colors pour in and out:
Here is a timeless structure wrought
Like the candelabrum of pure thought,
Stripped of green root and leaf,
Getting no seed to sprout,

Yet lovely, lovely,
God's Very Tree,
Form of whose intense inner life
Abstractly branches to attain
What glory, Tree, what pain?

Prophecy on Lethe

Echo, the beating of the tide,
Infringes on the blond curved shore;
Archaic weeds from sleep's green side
Bind skull and pelvis till the four
Seasons of the blood are unified.

Anonymous sweet carrion,
Blind mammal floating on the stream
Of depthless sound, completely one
In the cinnamon-dark of no dream—
A pod of silence, bursting when the sun

Clings to the forehead, will surprise
The gasping turtle and the leech
With your strange brain blooming as it lies
Abandoned to the bipeds on the beach;
Your jelly-mouth and, crushed, your polyp eyes.

LOVERS RELENTLESSLY

Lovers relentlessly contend to be
Superior in their identity:

The compass of the ego is designed
To circumscribe intact a lesser mind

With definition; tender thought would wrest
Each clean protective secret from the breast;

Affection's eyes go deep, make morbid lesion
In pride's tissue, are ferocious with possession;

Love's active hands are desperate to own
The subtly reasoned flesh on branching bone;

Lovers regard the simple moon that spills
White magic in a garden, bend their wills

Obliquely on each other; lovers eat
The small ecstatic heart to be complete;

Engaged in exquisite analysis
Of passionate destruction, lovers kiss;

In furious involvement they would make
A double meaning single. Some must break

Upon the wheel of love, but not the strange,
The secret lords, whom only death can change.

NOCTURNE

A leopard no more secret
Is than she who goes
By night alone, observing
Moon-foam upon the rose;

A doe is not more gentle
Than she who palely treads
Through peonies' white clusters,
Brushing small rabbit-heads;

Her steps are light as dew drops
Among imagined sheep,
Timid that she may startle
A herd of rocks from sleep;

She tarries for a moment
Beside a sky-deep pond
To watch a floating turtle;
Enchanted, moves beyond

To greet a glittering forest,
A tall and starry town
That calls to her supple body,
"Come down! Come down!"

FOR PROSERPINE

Our purple tongues that testify
The pomegranate has been broken
Are stained, their roots and buds are stained, with the shy
Fruity pleasure of us, met, spoken.

(I shall remember the days
Of my youth and your beautiful new ways.)

In fierce decay I'll find a stripe
Of honey sweetening the tart
Old brain. But shall I know again such ripe
Beauty of the burst, dark heart?

(I'll think of my absurd,
Impossible, pledged, serious word.)

PARTING

Parting, I take with me completed June,
My treasury of time, hoarded intact;
Eventual winds will not dissolve a tune
Of solid air, the body of this fact.
Mind's acres are forever green: Oh, I
Shall keep perpetual summer here; I shall
Refuse to let one startled swallow die,
Or, from the copper beeches, one leaf fall.

Here, vagrant from confusion, I shall greet
My youth immaculate in memory's urn;
This is my country, where the tireless feet
Of my adventure, homing, will return.
Each day will end in this day; every ship
Will bring me back, bright lip on lonely lip.

I Dreamed That I Was Old

I dreamed that I was old: in stale declension
Fallen from my prime, when company
Was mine, cat-nimbleness, and green invention,
Before time took my leafy hours away.

My wisdom, ripe with body's ruin, found
Itself tart recompense for what was lost
In false exchange: since wisdom in the ground
Has no apocalypse or pentecost.

I wept for my youth, sweet passionate young thought,
And cozy women dead that by my side
Once lay: I wept with bitter longing, not
Remembering how in my youth I cried.

NIGHT-PIECE

And everywhere, all over, men have sighed
Good night, remembering of women the bright
Of eyes; put out their bodies like a light,
And set their brains adrift upon their blood.

Let us be shy again like feathered things,
Stroll in the gardens of the spectrum (all
Last summer); waiting for the first snowfall,
Hear colors dropping, and the brisk flurry of wings.

Prevent that deepmost dream. Think late, think soon,
Of crickets, Marvell, roses, and the bare
Shoulders of teasing Venus, and oh the hair
Tumbling all over, everywhere, the moon.

Up ever so many stairs it is a new
Sweet (look! it's) morning in each other's arms.
Tell me, yes I truly, by what charms
Have I been, darling, yes I really do.

So bear with me, and if I thrash and groan
In the throes of sleep, believe me that I saw
The great fish tunneling the purple sea,
Earth-darkening bird that harries man alone.

Between Me and the Rock

Endlessly to no end wending
Pilgrim O my conscience in the green
Nacre of twilight abbreviate the heart

Autumn's beak is to the south
Death is north; westward one minute late
The plumed train leaps the shrilly stark ravine
Ever go feet go cars go the planes

Hearing the motors of the breast the brain
Loudly I wait their destinations wait

Coals of remembrance kissed and broken
These are the eyes; treasure the moment pure
Arrived at beauty impossible and vain

Now between me and the rock is
Now between me and myself is
Sight of the rock thought of myself: division sure

Then will the mouth of the air open
Cold slowly desolation pour over the blind
Punctures of sleep great gorges of the mind
Render me imperturbable to the rock
Deliver to myself completely me

TRANSFORMATIONS

All night he ran, his body air,
But that was in another year.

Lately the answered shape of his laughter,
The shape of his smallest word, is fire.

He who is a fierce young crier
Of poems will be tranquil as water,

Keeping, in sunset glow, the pure
Image of limitless desire;

Then enter earth and come to be,
Inch by inch, geography.

FIRST LOVE

At his incipient sun
The ice of twenty winters broke,
Crackling, in her eyes.

Her mirroring, still mind,
That held the world (made double) calm,
Turned fluid, and it ran.

There was a stir of music,
Mixed with flowers, in her blood;
A swift impulsive balm

From obscure roots;
Gold bees of clinging light
Swarmed in her brow.

Her throat is full of songs,
She hums, she is sensible of wings
Growing on her heart.

She is a tree in spring
Trembling with the hope of leaves,
Of which the leaves are tongues.

LAST WORDS

Listen: from sleep's long pillow I arise
To go away. One moment let me lean
On falling air before I lock my eyes.
Are the leaves red now? No matter. Trees are green.

The colors of the world are permanent
Despite the bleach of change. Pure stain on stain,
The bow of light's eternal forms is bent
Across steep heaven in the general brain.

Who cries, The beautiful, the proud, are fallen?
(O silly child, it was myself that cried.)
Death, eater of the heads of flowers, spills pollen:
Our little strength, our beauty, and our pride

Are for the race to keep; we can discover
Secrets with our broken skulls; our dead feet run
Under the lid of earth that closes over
The generations marching to the sun.

EAGLE

The dwindling pole,
Tall perpendicular in air,
Attenuates to be a bird
Poised on a sphere.

No flag projects
This tensile grace, this needle-word,
Only, in rigid attitude,
The ball, the bird.

Metallic time
Has caught an eagle, trapped the beat
Of rushing wings, ensnared in bronze
His taloned feet.

Invader of
The thunder, never will you fly
Again to pluck the blazing heart.
Shall I? Shall I?

So Intricately
Is This World Resolved

So intricately is this world resolved
Of substance arched on thrust of circumstance,
The earth's organic meaning so involved
That none may break the pattern of his dance;
Lest, deviating, he confound the line
Of reason with the destiny of race,
And, altering the perilous design,
Bring ruin like a rain on time and space.

Lover, it is good to lie in the sweet grass
With a dove-soft nimble girl. But O lover,
Lift no destroying hand; let fortune pass
Unchallenged, beauty sleep; dare not to cover
Her mouth with kisses by the garden wall,
Lest, cracking in bright air, a planet fall.

BENEDICTION

God banish from your house
The fly, the roach, the mouse

That riots in the walls
Until the plaster falls;

Admonish from your door
The hypocrite and liar;

No shy, soft, tigrish fear
Permit upon your stair,

Nor agents of your doubt.
God drive them whistling out.

Let nothing touched with evil,
Let nothing that can shrivel

Heart's tenderest frond, intrude
Upon your still, deep blood.

Against the drip of night
God keep all windows tight,

Protect your mirrors from
Surprise, delirium,

Admit no trailing wind
Into your shuttered mind

To plume the lake of sleep
With dreams. If you must weep

God give you tears, but leave
You secrecy to grieve,

And islands for your pride,
And love to nest in your side.

IN A STRANGE HOUSE

The memory of time is here imprisoned
In these walls, not fluent time that moves
Upon the flood, but time already reasoned
And undone of its quick eyes and loves.

We who are strangers in this finished house
Have slept with tossing shadows, and we lie
Astonished in our chambers lest we rouse
The strong assassins with a cry.

The dead would murder action. Oh, I know
Their subtle ways. They separate with fear
The fiery lips of thought. And I shall go
By silent lanes and leave you timeless here.

MASTER AND MISTRESS

As if I were composed of dust and air,
The shape confronting me upon the stair
(Athlete of shadow, lighted by a stain
On its disjunctive breast—I saw it plain—)
Moved through my middle flesh. I turned around,
Shaken, and it was marching without sound
Beyond the door; and when my hand was taken
From my mouth to beat the standing heart, I cried
My distant name, thinking myself had died.
One moment I was entered; one moment then
I knew a total century of pain
Between the twinkling of two thoughts. The ghost
Knocked on my ribs, demanding, "Host! Host!
I am diseased with motion. Give me bread
Before I quickly go. Shall I be fed?"
Yielding, I begged of him: "Partake of me.
Whatever runneth from the artery,
This body and its unfamiliar wine,
Stored in whatever dark of love, are thine."
But he denied me, saying, "Every part
Of thee is given, yea, thy flesh, thy heart."

ORGANIC BLOOM

The brain constructs its systems to enclose
The steady paradox of thought and sense;
Momentously its tissued meaning grows
To solve and integrate experience.
But life escapes closed reason. We explain
Our chaos into cosmos, cell by cell,
Only to learn of some insidious pain
Beyond the limits of our charted hell,
A guilt not mentioned in our prayers, a sin
Conceived against the self. So, vast and vaster
The plasmic circles of gray discipline
Spread outward to include each new disaster.
Enormous floats the brain's organic bloom
Till, bursting like a fruit, it scatters doom.

BEYOND REASON

The blessing in this conscious fruit, the hurt
Which is unanswerable, fill the brow
With early death. O Sion of my heart,
The milk of love were charitable now.

I do not come intent to be your lord,
Nor to contract the empire of your flight,
But as the long eye holds the spinning bird
Enclosed in the circumference of sight

And yet the bird is infinitely free
To dip its beak into the thinnest air,
So do I stand. I am not destiny
To color time or plot a hemisphere.

Creatures that carry in their little blood
Malignant influences moved to keep
Delight from love, the lonely from the proud,
Destroy themselves to live. If in my sleep

The ape, the serpent, and the fox I find
Shut with my soul in fortune's writhing sack,
I tame them with the sections of my mind
And teach my mind to love its thoughtless crack.

THE LESSON

Observe the wisdom of the Florentine
Who, feeling death upon him, scribbled fast
To make revision of a deathbed scene,
Gloating that he was accurate at last.

Let sons learn from their lipless fathers how
Man enters hell without a golden bough.

Vita Nuova

I abdicate my daily self that bled,
As others breathe, for porridge it might sup.
Henceforth apocalypse will get my bread
For me. I bit my tongue and gnawed my lip,
But now the visor of my name is up.

So I will peel that vision from my brain
Of numbers wrangling in a common place,
And I will go, unburdened, on the quiet lane
Of my eternal kind, till shadowless
With inner light I wear my father's face.

Moon of the soul, accompany me now,
Shine on the colosseums of my sense,
Be in the tabernacles of my brow.
My dark will make, reflecting from your stones,
The single beam of all my life intense.

PASSPORT TO THE WAR

Cities shall suffer siege and some shall fall,
But man's not taken. What the deep heart means,
Its message of the big, round, childish hand,
Its wonder, its simple lonely cry,
The bloodied envelope addressed to you,
Is history, that wide and mortal pang.

1944

REFLECTION BY A MAILBOX

When I stand in the center of that man's madness,
Deep in his trauma, as in the crater of a wound,
My ancestors step from my American bones.
There's mother in a woven shawl, and that,
No doubt, is father picking up his pack
For the return voyage through those dreadful years
Into the winter of the raging eye.

One generation past, two days by plane away,
My house is dispossessed, my friends dispersed,
My teeth and pride knocked in, my people game
For the hunters of man-skins in the warrens of Europe,
The impossible creatures of an hysteriac's dream
Advancing with hatchets sunk into their skulls
To rip the god out of the machine.

Are these the citizens of the new estate
To which the continental shelves aspire;
Or the powerful get of a dying age, corrupt
And passion-smeared, with fluid on their lips,
As if a soul had been given to petroleum?

How shall we uncreate that lawless energy?

Now I wait under the hemlock by the road
For the red-haired postman with the smiling hand
To bring me my passport to the war.
Familiarly his car shifts into gear
Around the curve; he coasts up to my drive; the day
Strikes noon; I think of Pavlov and his dogs
And the motto carved on the broad lintel of his brain:
"Sequence, consequence, and again consequence."

THE LAST PICNIC

The guests in their summer colors have fled
Through field and hedgerow. Come, let's pick
The bones and feathers of our fun
And kill the fire with a savage stick.

The figures of our country play,
The mocking dancers, in a swirl
Of laughter waved from the evening's edge,
Wrote finis to a pastoral.

Now the tongue of the military man,
Summoning the violent,
Calls the wild dogs out of their holes
And the deep Indian from his tent,

Not to be tamed, not to be stamped
Under. Earth-faced, behind this grove,
Our failures creep with soldier hearts,
Pointing their guns at what we love.

When they shall paint our sockets gray
And light us like a stinking fuse,
Remember that we once could say,
Yesterday we had a world to lose.

WELCOME THE WRATH

Poor john, who joined in make of wrong
And guessed no guile, dare I complain?—
Or practice to endure the heart unstrung,
The waiting at the door too long,
Winter, wages, and self-disdain.

Endure? That is the dialect of love,
The greenhorn of the west, my late companion,
Now straggling crossfoot half-alive
Back to his country, with crazy sleeve
Flopping, like a shot pinion.

Let him endure. I'll not: not warp my vision
To square with odds; not scrape; not scamp my fiber,
Though pushed by spoilers of the nerves' precision,
Bothered by caterpillars of suspicion,
Hired by speculators in my gut and labor.

Wrath has come down from the hills to enlist
Me surely in his brindled generation,
The race of the tiger; come down at last
Has wrath to build a bonfire of these rags
With one wet match and all man's desolation.

NIGHT LETTER

The urgent letter that I try to write
Night after night to you to whom I turn,
The staunchless word, my language of the wound,
Begins to stain the page. Here in my room
With my unkenneled need, the Faustian dog
That chews my penitential bones, I hope
And do not hope, I pray and mock my prayer,
Twisting my coils, this dangling life of mine,
Now twelve years come of age, and me unpleased
With all my ways, my very littlest ones,
My part, my lines, unless you hold them dear.
Where is your ministry? I thought I heard
A piece of laughter break upon the stair
Like glass, but when I wheeled around I saw
Disorder, in a tall magician's hat,
Keeping his rabbit-madness crouched inside,
Sit at my desk and scramble all the news.
The strangest things are happening. Christ! the dead,
Pushing the membrane from their face, salute
The dead and scribble slogans on our walls;
Phantoms and phobias mobilize, thronging
The roads; and in the Bitch's streets the men
Are lying down, great crowds with fractured wills
Dumping the shapeless burden of their lives
Into the rivers where the motors flowed.

Of those that stood in my doorway, self-accused,
Besmeared with failure in the swamps of trade,
One put a gun in his examiner's hand,
Making the judgment loud; another squats

Upon the asylum floor and plays with toys,
Like the spiral of a soul balanced on a stone,
Or a new gadget for slicing off the thumb;
The rest whirl in the torment of our time.
What have we done to them that what they are
Shrinks from the touch of what they hoped to be?
"Pardon," I plead, clutching the fragile sleeve
Of my poor father's ghost returned to howl
His wrongs. I suffer the twentieth century,
The nerves of commerce wither in my arm;
Violence shakes my dreams; I am so cold,
Chilled by the persecuting wind abroad,
The oratory of the rodent's tooth,
The slaughter of the blue-eyed open towns,
And principle disgraced, and art denied.
My dear, is it too late for peace, too late
For men to gather at the wells to drink
The sweet water; too late for fellowship
And laughter at the forge; too late for us
To say, "Let us be good to one another"?
The lamps go singly out; the valley sleeps;
I tend the last light shining on the farms
And keep for you the thought of love alive,
As scholars dungeoned in an ignorant age
Tended the embers of the Trojan fire.
Cities shall suffer siege and some shall fall,
But man's not taken. What the deep heart means,
Its message of the big, round, childish hand,
Its wonder, its simple lonely cry,
The bloodied envelope addressed to you,
Is history, that wide and mortal pang.

FATHER AND SON

Now in the suburbs and the falling light
I followed him, and now down sandy road
Whiter than bone-dust, through the sweet
Curdle of fields, where the plums
Dropped with their load of ripeness, one by one.
Mile after mile I followed, with skimming feet,
After the secret master of my blood,
Him, steeped in the odor of ponds, whose indomitable love
Kept me in chains. Strode years; stretched into bird;
Raced through the sleeping country where I was young,
The silence unrolling before me as I came,
The night nailed like an orange to my brow.

How should I tell him my fable and the fears,
How bridge the chasm in a casual tone,
Saying, "The house, the stucco one you built,
We lost. Sister married and went from home,
And nothing comes back, it's strange, from where she goes.
I lived on a hill that had too many rooms:
Light we could make, but not enough of warmth,
And when the light failed, I climbed under the hill.
The papers are delivered every day;
I am alone and never shed a tear."

At the water's edge, where the smothering ferns lifted
Their arms, "Father!" I cried, "Return! You know
The way. I'll wipe the mudstains from your clothes;
No trace, I promise, will remain. Instruct
Your son, whirling between two wars,
In the Gemara of your gentleness,

For I would be a child to those who mourn
And brother to the foundlings of the field
And friend of innocence and all bright eyes.
O teach me how to work and keep me kind."

Among the turtles and the lilies he turned to me
The white ignorant hollow of his face.

THE HEMORRHAGE

The people made a ring
Around the man in the park.
He was our banished king
Of blames and staunchless flows,
Exhibitor of the dark
Abominable rose;

Our chief, returned at last
From exile, with the grim
Stamina of the lost,
To show his sovereign hurt.
Wildly we dreaded him
And the strong god of his heart

Escaping, crawling down
Ditches where papers blow,
Smearing the sills of the town,
Strangling the hydra-drains
Coiled under. Stop! We know
How much a man contains.

We picnicked all that day,
Dishonored signs that nayed us,
Pulled marigolds, were gay
Before the apes, smashed glass.
Rifles could not have made us
Keep off the bloody grass;

For we were sick of crimes
Against us, and the head
Pitched on the absorbing Times,
And no one to accuse,
And nothing paid for, and we read,
We read that day what blotted out the news.

THE HARSH JUDGMENT

Inside, a hundred doors by which to leave;
Outside, you never can come in again.
The gesture made is woven in the sleeve,
The spiral echo sinks into the grain.
What died in me will warn me if you turn
Not to be tender-minded, though I burn,
In time so cruel, so difficult for love.

The burden of the personal, the life
By profit plowed, the tapping of our power—
You know the long rebellion and the spleen.
Last night, last year, with the tumbling of a leaf
The autumn came. Dark leaf from darker tower
Falls miles, deeper than coals, and still goes down.
Courage! That pity made our hearts unclean.

CONFIDENTIAL INSTRUCTIONS

When, on your dangerous mission gone,
You underrate our foes as dunces,
Be wary, not of sudden gun,
But of your partner at the dances;

Lest you be tamed in dead-end alleys
Where the mind's virtue drops from sight,
Loath to unlink from darling follies
Cuddled in houses of deceit;

Or cozened dearly by the bitch
Of souls, the international spy
Whirling in young men's arms, to each
Mistress, but in old carrion's pay.

THE SIGNAL FROM THE HOUSE

I said to the watcher at the gate,
"They also kill who wait."

I cried to the mourner on the stair,
"Mother, I hate you for those tears."

To mistress of the ruined hall,
The keeper of the sacred heart,

I brought the mind's indifference
And the heavy marble of my face.

For these who were too much with me
Were secretly against me:

Hostages to the old life,
Expecting to be ransomed daily

And for the same fond reason
From the deep prison of their person,

Their lantern shining in the window
Had signaled me, like cry of conscience,

Insisting that I must be broken
Upon the wheel of the unforsaken.

THE TUTORED CHILD

Your mother, whom the mirror-world has claimed,
Plucks at the telltale hairs with violent hand
And thinks time backward to a brassy song,
Rolling the grape of hysteria under her tongue.

Your father, in whom two ambitions rave,
Like stations wrangling on the foreign wave
For spheres of influence, loathes the heart that blends
His guilty love; but the quarrel never ends.

You are of nature's bright unlucky brood,
Born of the drop of talent in your blood
Wherewith the gates of mystery are oiled.
Mortals will touch you and your taste be spoiled,

Witches in metals test you. I observe
Defeat, taking short cuts from nerve to nerve,
Climb through the narrow transom of your will;
And I weep, for having made you vulnerable.

My poor poor child whose terrors never cease,
Here is my pity penny. Buy you peace.

THE ECONOMIST'S SONG

Come sit beneath the tariff walls
Among the scuttling unemployed,
The rodent pack; sing madrigals
Of Demos and the Cyprian maid
Bewildered by the golden grain,
While ships with peril in their hulls,
Deploying on the lines of trade,
Transport the future of gangrene.

THE OLD CLOTHES MAN

Have you any old clothes to sell?
The years make a stain you can't conceal,
Your fabric's eaten, you discard
That part of your life for which you cared.

You pluck a thread from your cuff: it winces
Straight to your shoulder. Ambition grieves
In trunks and bags; moth-featured, minces
From closets, beating empty sleeves.

History stagnates in your house.
I smelt the ruinous time, will buy
Your waste of talent. There's an ooze
Of souls too virulent to die

Contagious on the baffling walls.
You sit and watch the ceiling crack;
Horror sifts through and softly falls
From worlds beyond the zodiac.

You fear the unappeasable bone
That growls in your breast, and the mind's long feather,
The heart that imitates a stone
Until your hands grow fast together

And violence unstrings your voice.
I know what hangs behind your stair,
Spoiling with conscience and disuse:
The uniform you never wear,

The fitness and the pride, so vilely
Dishonored, the smiling target mouth,
Innocence ambushed, in the sharp volley
Reeling before the huntsmen of youth.

Therefore I come to mobilize
Your poor blind wounds, as in the coat,
The form betrayed, the defeated eyes,
My brother my groom, my dear recruit.

There will be skirmishing and loot
And fires to light our marches. Let
The enemies of life beware
When these old clothes go forth to war.

THE FITTING OF THE MASK

"Again I come to buy the image fated."
"Your valued image, sir, and that's a pity,
Is gone, I mean the youth, the undefeated,
Whose falcon-heart, winged with the golden shout
Of morning, sweeps windward from his native city,
Crying his father's grief, his mother's doubt."

"You knew I cared, and that I'd come for him;
The traffic hindered me; you should have known."
"Ah there, that's bad! But my poor memory's dim
As a bell that rings the tide in; I lose track
Of things to keep and things to sell, and one
Can never be quite certain who'll come back."

"Enough! There was another face, a bright
Pathetic one I'll take, from whose wild stain
Of sympathy a man could borrow light."
"Our catalogue describes him 'Fool of Love,
Fragile and dear, tinctured with mortal pain,
Buys grain of his grain and eats the chaff thereof.' "

"Your cataloguer has the cynic touch,
But I'll forgive him. Is our business over?"
"Be patient, sir. You would not thank me much
Or recommend my baffling merchandise
If I should offer this unblessed believer,
This torn-cheek, with the chasm in his eyes."

"Old man, I'm in a hurry to proceed,
And everyone, you know, must wear a mask.

Give me a countenance to meet my need
Or malice will expose me at the dance."
"Oh sir, we'll try, but it's no easy task
To make adjustments to your circumstance;

And now, while my assistant turns the key
And in the windows now the lights go out,
For it is closing time irrevocably
Until new features sit upon the forms,
I'll sing a little ditty to the ghost
That occupies this world of empty frames.

[*Sings:*]
Good-fellow's lost among our Psychic Cases,
The Angry Man has turned a ghastly blue,
Munich exhausted all our Judas-faces,
And what are we to do, and what to do?
The Optimist was mangled in a sock,
The rats conferred and ate The Wandering Jew,
There's nothing left that's decent in our stock,
And what are we to do, and what to do?

But look!——here's something rare, macabre, a true
Invention of the time's insomniac wits.
Perhaps we ought to sell it to the zoo.
Go to the darkening glass that traps your shames
And tell me what you see."
                              "O Prince of Counterfeits,
This is the Self I hunted and knifed in dreams!"

THE SUPPER BEFORE LAST

The intellectuals at the feast,
Emaciated on their fare,
Clap hands at the fabulous new beast
Upon the massive platter borne.
Their tongues rejoice, steeped in the rare
Juices of the unicorn;
While drunk with ptomaines now, the crow
That hoarsely to the table came,
Snatches at gobbets flung below,
And smirking in his greasy frock
Clamps beak on the honeyed mortal game
Under the dreaming hip and hock.

THE DAUGHTERS OF
THE HORSELEECH

The daughters of the horseleech crying "Give! Give!"
Implore the young men for the blood of martyrs.
How shall we keep the old senator alive
Unless we satisfy his thirst for cultures?

Entreat the rat, the weasel, and the fox
To forage for a toothless master;
Have mercy, boys, on the monkey in his box;
Dear Judas goat, lead out the sheep to slaughter,

For if the warlock with the gilded claws
Withers away, and of his bones are waters,
Who will transmute our foreheads into brass
And who will keep his two charming daughters?

CARELESS LOVE

Who have been lonely once
Are comforted by their guns.
Affectionately they speak
To the dark beauty, whose cheek
Beside their own cheek glows.
They are calmed by such repose,
Such power held in hand;
Their young bones understand
The shudder in that frame.
Without nation, without name,
They give the load of love,
And it's returned, to prove
How much the husband heart
Can hold of it: for what
This nymphomaniac enjoys
Inexhaustibly is boys.

THE GUILTY MAN

The years of my life were odd that now are even.
Think! to be young, amused, and not a fool;
Playing the world's game—think!—with world's own rules,
And nothing lost, I think, I think . . . but years.
Heart against mouth is singing out of tune,
Night's whisperings and blanks betrayed; this is
The end of lies: my bones are angry with me.

Father, the darkness of the self goes out
And spreads contagion on the flowing air.
I walk obscurely in a cloud of dark:
Yea, when I kneeled, the dark kneeled down with me.
Touch me: my folds and my defenses fall;
I stand within myself, myself my shield.

Between the Acts

Fate hired me once to play a villain's part.
I did it badly, wasting valued blood;
Now when the call is given to the good,
It is that knave who answers in my heart.

THIS DAY THIS WORLD

My architects, forsaking me,
Submit designs for a bombproof mansion;
My scholars of the fourth dimension
Complain they starve to death in three;
My correspondents write all day
The business of the enemy.

Tapped of their useful energies,
My soldiers pace the mind's frontier;
Engine recoils from engineer
And strikes at the courage in his eyes.
When shall my swarthy workmen rise,
Demand the power and the keys?

THE LAST QUESTION

Oh the good times! the laughter on the hill!
The parties down at Larry's in the spring!
Your sovereign pleasure, careless itself to save,
Goes naked at the heart. Touching, you bring
Rumors of heaven and its generous spoils
Here, even, where our hooded shadows rise
To play the stab-scene, the end of love,
While grief intones, ever the third that stays.
Now that your pity shines in other hall,
Now that your grain again comes to the mill,
Shall I be happy soon, shall I rejoice,
Or wrestle with that stranger whom you praise?

How Long Is the Night?

On the anvil of love my flesh has been hammered out.
Indifferent, in the indifferent air,
I circulate and suck the star-space in.
No one is dear to me now,
Leastly myself that sickened in the night.
I would abandon this loose bag of bones
And walk between the world's great wounds, unpitying.

THE RECKONING
"What have you done?"

Pigeon, who are to me
Language and light
And the long flight home,
Your question comes with coils
Like years behind,
Which I am crawling from.
Be patient with my wound:
Too long I lay
In the folds of my preparation,
Sinuous in the sun,
A golden skin,
All pride, sores, excretion,
Blazing with death. O child,
From my angry side
Tumbles this agate heart,
Your prize, veined with the root
Of guilty life,
From which flow love and art.

OPEN THE GATES

Within the city of the burning cloud,
Dragging my life behind me in a sack,
Naked I prowl, scourged by the black
Temptation of the blood grown proud.

Here at the monumental door,
Carved with the curious legend of my youth,
I brandish the great bone of my death,
Beat once therewith and beat no more.

The hinges groan: a rush of forms
Shivers my name, wrenched out of me.
I stand on the terrible threshold, and I see
The end and the beginning in each other's arms.

FROM

THIS GARLAND, DANGER

I listen, I am always listening,
In fear that something might get by,
To the grammar of the public places,
But I fly toward Possibility,
In the extravagantly gay
Surprise of a journey,
Careless that I am bound
To the flaming wheel of my bones.

IN
SELECTED POEMS: 1928–1958

THE SCIENCE OF THE NIGHT

I touch you in the night, whose gift was you,
My careless sprawler,
And I touch you cold, unstirring, star-bemused,
That have become the land of your self-strangeness.
What long seduction of the bone has led you
Down the imploring roads I cannot take
Into the arms of ghosts I never knew,
Leaving my manhood on a rumpled field
To guard you where you lie so deep
In absent-mindedness,
Caught in the calcium snows of sleep?

And even should I track you to your birth
Through all the cities of your mortal trial,
As in my jealous thought I try to do,
You would escape me—from the brink of earth
Take off to where the lawless auroras run,
You with your wild and metaphysic heart.
My touch is on you, who are light-years gone.
We are not souls but systems, and we move
In clouds of our unknowing
                              like great nebulae.
Our very motives swirl and have their start
With father lion and with mother crab.
Dreamer, my own lost rib,
Whose planetary dust is blowing
Past archipelagoes of myth and light,
What far Magellans are you mistress of
To whom you speed the pleasure of your art?
As through a glass that magnifies my loss

I see the lines of your spectrum shifting red,
The universe expanding, thinning out,
Our worlds flying, oh flying, fast apart.

From hooded powers and from abstract flight
I summon you, your person and your pride.
Fall to me now from outer space,
Still fastened desperately to my side;
Through gulfs of streaming air
Bring me the mornings of the milky ways
Down to my threshold in your drowsy eyes;
And by the virtue of your honeyed word
Restore the liquid language of the moon,
That in gold mines of secrecy you delve.
Awake!
          My whirling hands stay at the noon,
Each cell within my body holds a heart
And all my hearts in unison strike twelve.

GREEN WAYS

Let me not say it, let me not reveal
How like a god my heart begins to climb
The trellis of the crystal
In the rose-green moon;
Let me not say it, let me leave untold
This legend, while the nights snow emerald.

Let me not say it, let me not confess
How in the leaflight of my green-celled world
In self's pre-history
The blind moulds kiss;
Let me not say it, let me but endure
This ritual like feather and like star.

Let me proclaim it—human be my lot!—
How from my pit of green horse-bones
I turn, in a wilderness of sweat,
To the moon-breasted sibylline,
And lift this garland, Danger, from her throat
To blaze it in the foundries of the night.

WHEN THE LIGHT FALLS

When the light falls, it falls on her
In whose rose-gilded chamber
A music strained through mind
Turns everything to measure.

The light that seeks her out
Finds answering light within,
And the two join hands and dance
On either side of her skin.

The lily and the swan
Attend her whiter pride,
While the courtly laurel kneels
To kiss his mantling bride.

Under each cherry-bough
She spreads her silken cloths
At the rumor of a wind,
To gather up her deaths,

For the petals of her heart
Are shaken in a night,
Whose ceremonial art
Is dying into light.

AMONG THE GODS

Within the grated dungeon of the eye
The old gods, shaggy with gray lichen, sit
Like fragments of the antique masonry
Of heaven, a patient thunder in their stare.

Huge blocks of language, all my quarried love,
They justify, and not in random poems,
But shapes of things interior to Time,
Hewn out of chaos when the Pure was plain.

Sister, my bride, who were both cloud and bird
When Zeus came down in a shower of sexual gold,
Listen! we make a world! I hear the sound
Of Matter pouring through eternal forms.

AS FLOWERS ARE

As flowers have wars that the philosophic eye
Stoops to behold, broils of the golden age
When honey dropped from the trees, and the bees perform
Their educated dance, we find our skins
In which to parable the act of love,
Contending, as at first, that the world might move.

Perfection caught in amber of our days
Jewels the life; on the offended thread
We hang the instants of the soul's surprise
When it is ravished by the absolute god,
Who comes in any shape that he may choose
But the expected one: as flowers tell lies.

Your lazy tongue that makes me think of bells
And soft Mediterranean afternoons
(As flowers shoot stars) rings out its heaven-changes
Till souls and gods pick clover in your lines
And what I carry through the giant grass
Mocks the profession of the comic ants.

Summer is late, my heart: the dusty fiddler
Hunches under the stone; these pummelings
Of scent are more than masquerade; I have heard
A song repeat, repeat, till my breath had failed.
As flowers have flowers, at the season's height,
A single color oversweeps the field.

The Waltzer in the House

A sweet, a delicate white mouse,
A little blossom of a beast,
Is waltzing in the house
Among the crackers and the yeast.

O the swaying of his legs!
O the bobbing of his head!
The lady, beautiful and kind,
The blue-eyed mistress, lately wed,
Has almost laughed away her wits
To see the pretty mouse that sits
On his tiny pink behind
And swaying, bobbing, begs.

She feeds him tarts and curds,
Seed packaged for the birds,
And figs, and nuts, and cheese;
Polite as Pompadour to please
The dainty waltzer of her house,
The sweet, the delicate, the innocent white mouse.

As in a dream, as in a trance,
She loves his rhythmic elegance,
She laughs to see his bobbing dance.

SOTTO VOCE

Say to me only
Huntress of nerves
You too are lonely
For the language that saves

Heart be not alien
Come to me strange
In the breast of a felon
Whose prison is songs

Share with me always
Though fraction be cross
The instant of gallows
The kiss of the axe

GRAMMAR LESSON

Waking was laughing then,
Orations without words;
Wishing was present tense
And that meant motion towards.

"There's grammar in my bones!"
I parsed it slow and lazy;
Endearments came in pairs,
Making my homage easy;

Each substantive drank light,
Required no definition,
Embraced its opposite,
As even poet, nation;

Looking and liking twined,
Red lions dressed their loins,
The pockets of my sight
Jingled with brand-new coins

Till brightness, original day,
Creator-kissed, appeared,
With the usual angel, stiff,
Waving his guttural sword—

But how could I remember
So early in the morning
(I lucky in my bed
And loved) Old Adverb's warning?

SHE WEPT, SHE RAILED

She wept, she railed, she spurned the meat
Men toss into a muslin cage
To make their spineless doxy bleat
For pleasure and for patronage,
As if she had no choice but eat
The lewd bait of a squalid age.

That moment when the lights go out
The years shape to the sprawling thing,
A marmoset with bloodied clout,
A pampered flank that learns to sing,
Without the grace, she cried, to doubt
The postures of the underling.

I thought of Judith in her tent,
Of Helen by the crackling wall,
Of Cressida, her bone-lust spent,
Of Catherine on the holy wheel:
I heard their woman-dust lament
The golden wound that does not heal.

What a wild air her small joints beat!
I only poured the raging wine
Until our bodies filled with light,
Mine with hers and hers with mine,
And we went out into the night
Where all the constellations shine.

FOREIGN AFFAIRS

We are two countries girded for the war,
Whisking our scouts across the pricked frontier
To ravage in each other's fields, cut lines
Along the lacework of strategic nerves,
Loot stores; while here and there,
In ambushes that trace a valley's curves,
Stark witness to the dangerous charge we bear,
A house ignites, a train's derailed, a bridge
Blows up sky-high, and water floods the mines.
Who first attacked? Who turned the other cheek?
Aggression perpetrated is as soon
Denied, and insult rubbed into the injury
By cunning agents trained in these affairs,
With whom it's touch-and-go, don't-tread-on-me,
I-dare-you-to, keep-off, and kiss-my-hand.
Tempers could sharpen knives, and do; we live
In states provocative
Where frowning headlines scare the coffee cream
And doomsday is the eighth day of the week.

Our exit through the slammed and final door
Is twenty times rehearsed, but when we face
The imminence of cataclysmic rupture,
A lesser pride goes down upon its knees.
Two countries separated by desire!—
Whose diplomats speed back and forth by plane,
Portmanteaus stuffed with fresh apologies
Outdated by events before they land.
Negotiations wear them out: they're driven mad
Between the protocols of tears and rapture.

Locked in our fated and contiguous selves,
These worlds that too much agitate each other,
Interdependencies from hip to head,
Twin principalities both slave and free,
We coexist, proclaiming Peace together.
Tell me no lies! We are divided nations
With malcontents by thousands in our streets,
These thousands torn by inbred revolutions.
A triumph is demanded, not moral victories
Deduced from small advances, small retreats.
Are the gods of our fathers not still daemonic?
On the steps of the Capitol
The outraged lion of our years roars panic,
And we suffer the guilty cowardice of the will,
Gathering its bankrupt slogans up for flight
Like gold from ruined treasuries.
And yet, and yet, although the murmur rises,
We are what we are, and only life surprises.

THE UNWITHERED GARLAND

Her grace is not of any part,
But selfhood's self, its very motion,
The mortal dream surprised by art
More effortless than wind or ocean,
All spirit flowing out to burn
The essence of its contradiction,
And give more light the more it turn.
Things are not only what they are:
They pass beyond themselves to learn
The tears of the particular.
If she go ranging out of sight
To suffer on a distant star
Her wounding by the infinite,
It is in answer to her law.
Who had of her the world's delight
And loved her for her sacred flaw
Loves her not less beyond his reach,
Still with the wonder that he saw
Alive. Perfectly to pray,
As the Fathers of the Desert teach,
He does not even try to pray.

THE MAN UPSTAIRS

The old man sick with boyhood fears,
Whose thin shanks ride the naked blast,
Intones; the gray somnambulist
Creaks down interminable stairs,
Dreaming my future as his past.

A flower withers in its vase,
A print detaches from the wall,
Beyond the last electric bill
Slow days are crumbling into days
Without the unction of farewell.

Tonight there suffers in my street
The passion of the silent clerk
Whose drowned face cries the windows dark
Where once the bone of mercy beat.
I turn; I perish into work.

O Magus with the leathern hand,
The wasted heart, the trailing star,
Time is your madness, which I share,
Blowing next winter into mind . . .
And love herself not there, not there.

THE APPROACH TO THEBES

In the zero of the night, in the lipping hour,
Skin-time, knocking-time, when the heart is pearled
And the moon squanders its uranian gold,
She taunted me, who was all music's tongue,
Philosophy's and wilderness's breed,
Of shifting shape, half jungle-cat, half-dancer,
Night's woman-petaled, lion-scented rose,
To whom I gave, out of a hero's need,
The dolor of my thrust, my riddling answer,
Whose force no lesser mortal knows. Dangerous?
Yes, as nervous oracles foretold
Who could not guess the secret taste of her:
Impossible wine! I came into the world
To fill a fate; am punished by my youth
No more. What if dog-faced logic howls
Was it art or magic multiplied my joy?
Nature has reasons beyond true or false.
We played like metaphysic animals
Whose freedom made our knowledge bold
Before the tragic curtain of the day:
I can bear the dishonor now of growing old.

Blinded and old, exiled, diseased, and scorned—
The verdict's bitten on the brazen gates,
For the gods grant each of us his lot, his term.
Hail to the King of Thebes!—my self, ordained
To satisfy the impulse of the worm,
Bemummied in those famous incestuous sheets,
The bloodiest flags of nations of the curse,
To be hung from the balcony outside the room

Where I encounter my most flagrant source.
Children, grandchildren, my long posterity,
To whom I bequeath the spiders of my dust,
Believe me, whatever sordid tales you hear,
Told by physicians or mendacious scribes,
Of beardless folly, consanguineous lust,
Fomenting pestilence, rebellion, war,
I come prepared, unwanting what I see,
But tied to life. On the royal road to Thebes
I had my luck, I met a lovely monster,
And the story's this: I made the monster me.

THE DARK AND THE FAIR

A roaring company that festive night;
The beast of dialectic dragged his chains,
Prowling from chair to chair in the smoking light,
While the snow hissed against the windowpanes.

Our politics, our science, and our faith
Were whiskey on the tongue; I, being rent
By the fierce divisions of our time, cried death
And death again, and my own dying meant.

Out of her secret life, that griffin-land
Where ivory empires build their stage, she came,
Putting in mine her small impulsive hand,
Five-fingered gift, and the palm not tame.

The moment clanged: beauty and terror danced
To the wild vibration of a sister-bell,
Whose unremitting stroke discountenanced
The marvel that the mirrors blazed to tell.

A darker image took this fairer form
Who once, in the purgatory of my pride,
When innocence betrayed me in a room
Of mocking elders, swept handsome to my side,

Until we rose together, arm in arm,
And fled together back into the world.
What brought her now, in the semblance of the warm,
Out of cold spaces, damned by colder blood?

That furied woman did me grievous wrong,
But does it matter much, given our years?
We learn, as the thread plays out, that we belong
Less to what flatters us than to what scars;

So, freshly turning, as the turn condones,
For her I killed the propitiatory bird,
Kissing her down. Peace to her bitter bones,
Who taught me the serpent's word, but yet the word.

THE THIEF

In a Roman tram, where the famous Roman mob,
Wrung from the bowels of the hippodrome,
Mauled into shape its many-elbowed god
To fight for exit through its civil wars,
Somebody Roman picked my pocket clean.
A pagan and a Christian curse on him!
Somebody Roman, may he find tonight
In the street of the serpents or the lion's mouth,
Strewn on a wine-soaked board,
More than he reached for, more than cash,
Green trumpeters, for whom the legions march
Through solid stone. (Meanwhile the Carthaginians
Play redskins in the ambush of the sea
To whom must be meted out the standard destruction:
It is a heavy responsibility.)
                              Let the *ladrone* sneer
As the leathered fold yields him my haunt of years,
The papers of a life I wanted lost,
Memos, addresses, the snapshot of a child,
To plague him through his alley nights until
He begs for mercy for the thing well-robbed.
Worlds in my pocket older than his own,
May they erupt on him like hissing gold,
Tooth of the pythoness, chimaera's scales,
Stones of the temple and Isaiah's beard—
Toss him, sweet furies, from Tarpeia's Rock!

More even than my purse,
And that's no laughing matter, it is my pride
That has been hurt: a fine Italian hand,

With its mimosa touch, has made me feel
Blind-skinned, indelicate, a fool Americano
Touring a culture like a grand museum,
People and statues interchangeable shows,
Perception blunted as one's syntax fails.

Why am I here? Some thirty years ago
A set of lantern slides I saw at school
Of these antiquities gave me an image
Of the rare serene that brimmed my eyes,
For nothing pleased me then in my legacy;
But the past that tempted me, the frozen pure,
Was a pedagogic lie. All's motion here,
And motion like emotion is impure,
A flower flawed by mutability,
Religion by its ruins, and yet thereby
More lovely and more graced, perhaps
More true. Still, still, the chariot wheels
Turn, the assassin motorcyclists charge,
Wolves prowl in the streets under arcades of bells,
Tiberius grovels through his dungeon halls
Dreaming of boy-sized fishes in his bath;
Behind the balcony of the Cardinal's palace,
Smelling the laureled Mamertine blood,
A baldpate awaits his rhetorical cue,
And the clouds drift
Through a triumph of broken columns.

Pick-pocket, pick-thank music plucks the strings
For the rag-madonna with perdurable babe
Most dolorously hallowing the square
Where Caesar walks three steps to meet Bernini,
Whose sumptuous art runs wild

From gate to gate, pausing in tiptoe-joy
Only to light a torch of fountains, to set
His tritons dancing, or at a blest façade
To cast up from his wrist a flight of angels,
Volute on volute, wing on climbing wing.
In the middle of my life I heard the waters playing.

Mater Cloaca, feast thee well, I pray,
On what has been subtracted from my fate—
Ten days of lectures, thirty days abroad:
In this excess that's Rome I'll not mope long,
Wearing my heart less Roman than baroque,
Though damn it all! I wish I'd lived in style,
Jogged in *carrozze* round and round the town,
Guzzled Spumante by the bucketful,
Bought wagons of daffodils to please my dear.
Now that I face the moment and the loss,
Driven to language on the Ides of March
Here in my blistered room
Where the wind flaps my ceiling like a sail
(A miracle, no doubt, to be left at that!)
I recognize the gods' capricious hand
And write this poem for money, rage, and love.

END OF SUMMER

An agitation of the air,
A perturbation of the light
Admonished me the unloved year
Would turn on its hinge that night.

I stood in the disenchanted field
Amid the stubble and the stones,
Amazed, while a small worm lisped to me
The song of my marrow-bones.

Blue poured into summer blue,
A hawk broke from his cloudless tower,
The roof of the silo blazed, and I knew
That part of my life was over.

Already the iron door of the north
Clangs open: birds, leaves, snows
Order their populations forth,
And a cruel wind blows.

GOOSE POND

Goose Pond's imaginable snows,
The fall of twenty years at once,
Like subtler moons reflect the rose
Decompositions of the sun.

A feather tumbling from a cloud
Scrolls thunders of the natural law;
The cattails rattle; cinnamon fern
Raises rag banners toward the thaw,

And early-footed ghost flowers scour
Through willow-dapplings to a cave
Where secrecy grows fur. Self burns
At the pulpits where Jack-preachers rave!

Now a sulky weather dogs the heart,
There is no bottom to the day,
The water lily's Chinese stalk
Drags heavy, as the white-lipped boy

Climbs from detritus of his birth,
The rusted hoop, the broken wheels,
The sunken boat of little worth,
Past balconies of limber eels

Until, along that marshy brink,
The spongy trails devoid of plan,
He meets his childhood beating back
To find what furies made him man.

THE DRAGONFLY

Fallen, so freshly fallen
From his estates of air,
He made on the gritty path
A five-inch funeral car,
New Hampshire's lesser dragon
In the grip of his kidnapers.
A triumph of *chinoiserie*
He seemed, in green and gold
Enameling, pin-brained,
With swizzle-stick for tail,
The breastplate gemmed between.
What a gallantry of pomp
In that royal spread of wings!—
Four leaves of thinnest mica,
Or, better, of the skin
Of water, if water had a skin.
Semaphores, at rest,
Of the frozen invisible,
They caught a glinting light
In the hairlines of their scripture
When a vagrom current stirred
And made them feign to flutter.
It was a slow progress,
A thing of fits and starts,
With bands of black attendants
Tugging at the wings
And under the crested feelers
At the loose-hinged head

(So many eyes he had, which were
The eyes?), still others pushing
From behind, where a pair
Of ornamental silks
That steered him in his flights
Gave tenuous pincer-hold.
Admire, I said to myself,
How he lords it over them,
Grounded though he may be
After his blue-sky transports;
But see how they honor him,
His servants at the feast,
In a passion of obsequies,
With chomping mandibles
And wildly waving forelegs
Telegraphing news abroad
Of their booty's worth; oh praise this
Consummate purity
Of the bestriding will!
In a scaled-down mythology
These myrmidons could stand
For the separate atoms of St. George
(Why not?). And fancy drove
Me on, my science kneeling
Before such witless tools,
To pay my tithe of awe
And read the resurrection-sign
In the motion of the death.
But then I saw,
When an imperceptible gust
Abruptly hoisted sails

And flipped my hero over . . .
In the reversal of the scene
I saw the sixfold spasm
Of his tucked-in claws,
The cry of writhing nerve-ends,
And down his membrane-length
A tide of gray pulsation.
I wheeled. The scorpion sun,
Stoking its belly-fires,
Exploded overhead, and the rain
Came down: scales, tortuous wires,
Flakings of green and gold.

THE WAR AGAINST THE TREES

The man who sold his lawn to standard oil
Joked with his neighbors come to watch the show
While the bulldozers, drunk with gasoline,
Tested the virtue of the soil
Under the branchy sky
By overthrowing first the privet-row.

Forsythia-forays and hydrangea-raids
Were but preliminaries to a war
Against the great-grandfathers of the town,
So freshly lopped and maimed.
They struck and struck again,
And with each elm a century went down.

All day the hireling engines charged the trees,
Subverting them by hacking underground
In grub-dominions, where dark summer's mole
Rampages through his halls,
Till a northern seizure shook
Those crowns, forcing the giants to their knees.

I saw the ghosts of children at their games
Racing beyond their childhood in the shade,
And while the green world turned its death-foxed page
And a red wagon wheeled,
I watched them disappear
Into the suburbs of their grievous age.

Ripped from the craters much too big for hearts
The club-roots bared their amputated coils,
Raw gorgons matted blind, whose pocks and scars
Cried Moon! on a corner lot
One witness-moment, caught
In the rear-view mirrors of the passing cars.

THE THING THAT EATS
THE HEART

The thing that eats the heart comes wild with years.
It died last night, or was it wounds before,
But somehow crawls around, inflamed with need,
Jingling its medals at the fang-scratched door.

We were not unprepared: with lamp and book
We sought the wisdom of another age
Until we heard the action of the bolt.
A little wind investigates the page.

No use pretending to the pitch of sleep;
By turnings we are known, our times and dates
Examined in the courts of either/or
While armless griefs mount lewd and headless doubts.

It pounces in the dark, all pity-ripe,
An enemy as soft as tears or cancer,
In whose embrace we fall, as to a sickness
Whose toxins in our cells cry sin and danger.

Hero of crossroads, how shall we defend
This creature-lump whose charity is art
When its own self turns Christian-cannibal?
The thing that eats the heart is mostly heart.

By Lamplight

Welcome, eccentric life,
Attracted to my star,
Let there be festival
Perverse and singular.
Let any drop of poison
Grow legs and crawl and eat:
The malice of unreason
A man can tolerate.
The stumblers and the clowns
Are wired with their will
To live, to live, to live:
They do not mean to kill.
Sweet beetles, comrade moths,
The bonfires in your head
Are neither coals of hell
Nor the rose in the marriage-bed.
I heard all summer long
(Dance, monsters, hairy forms!)
The idiot on the leaf
Babbling of dust and storms,
And in this rough heart made
A little thin-legged song
Out of my greening blood
To swell the night's harangue.

THE SCOURGE

My heart felt need to die,
Our dusty time had come;
I said, "Endure the lie,
The waste, the tedium."

My heart sank to his knees,
Schooled in the tragic style,
But I, being out of heart,
Whipped him another mile,

And not because I cared
To let that actor go,
But only that I feared
His eternal No, No, No.

Beyond the covered bridge
The crooked road turned wild;
He rose at the season's edge,
Passionate and defiled,

Plucking the remnant leaf
Stained with the only good,
While all my children leaped
Out of the glowing wood.

HERMETIC POEM

The secret my heart keeps
Flows into cracked cups.

No saucer can contain
This overplus of mine:

It glisters to the floor,
Lashing like lizard fire

And ramps upon the walls
Crazy with ruby ills.

Who enters by my door
Is drowned, burned, stung, and starred.

TO THE READER

—from Charles Baudelaire: "Au Lecteur"

Ignorance, error, cupidity, and sin
Possess our souls and exercise our flesh;
From force of habit we cultivate remorse
As beggars entertain and nurse their lice.

Our sins are stubborn. Cowards when contrite
We overstuff confession with our pains,
and when we're back again in human mire
Vile tears, we think, will wash away our stains.

Thrice-potent Satan in our cursèd bed
Lulls us to sleep, our spirit overkissed,
Until the precious metal of our will
Is vaporized—that cunning alchemist!

Who but the Devil pulls our waking-strings?
Abominations lure us to their side;
Each day we take another step to hell,
Descending through the stench, unhorrified.

Like an exhausted rake who mouths and chews
The martyrized breast of an old withered whore
We steal, in passing, whatever joys we can,
Squeezing the driest orange all the more.

Packed in our brains incestuous as worms
Our demons celebrate in drunken gangs,
And when we breathe, that hollow rasp is Death
Sliding invisibly down into our lungs.

If the dull canvas of our wretched life
Is unembellished with such pretty ware
As knives or poison, pyromania, rape,
It is because our soul's too weak to dare!

But in this den of jackals, monkeys, curs,
Scorpions, buzzards, snakes—this paradise
Of filthy beasts that screech, howl, grovel, grunt—
In this menagerie of mankind's vice

There's one supremely hideous and impure!
Soft-spoken, not the type to cause a scene,
He'd willingly make rubble of the earth
And swallow up creation in a yawn.

I mean *Ennui!* who in his hookah-dreams
Produces hangmen and real tears together.
How well you know this fastidious monster, reader,
—Hypocrite reader, you—my double! my brother!

THE WAY DOWN

I

Time swings her burning hands
I saw him going down
Into those mythic lands
Bearing his selfhood's gold,
A last heroic speck
Of matter in his mind
That ecstasy could not crack
Nor metaphysics grind.
I saw him going down
Veridical with bane
Where pastes of phosphor shine
To a cabin underground
Where his hermit father lives
Escaping pound by pound
From his breast-buckled gyves;
In his hermit father's coat,
The coat without a seam,
That the race, in its usury, bought
For the agonist to redeem,
By dying in it, one
Degree a day till the whole
Circle's run.

2

When the magician died, I wept,
I also died, I under leaf forgot
The stars, the distaff, and the crystal bowl.
I hugged the ignorance of stone

Under the line of the crickets' thunder
Where the white chariot of the winter sun
Raced to the axle pole.
Why am I suddenly warm all over?
By the small mouths of the rain
I'm tempted. Must I learn again to breathe?
Help me, my worldlings, leave
To the hoot owl in the dismal wood
His kingdom of blight
And empty branching halls.
Air thickens to dirt.
Great hairy seeds that soar aloft
Like comets trailing tender spume
Break in the night with soft
Explosions into bloom.
Where the fleshed root stirs,
Marvelous horned strong game,
Brine-scaled, dun-caked with mould,
Dynastic thunder-bison, Asian-crude,
Bedded in moss and slime,
Wake, and the rhythm of their blood
Shoots through the long veins of my name.
Hail, thickets! Hail, dark stream!

3

Time swings her burning hands.
The blossom is the fruit,
And where I walk, the leaves
Lie level with the root.
My brave god went from me.
I saw him going down
Incorrigibly wild

In a cloud of golden air.
O father in the wood,
Mad father of us all,
King of our antlered wills,
Our candelabrum-pride
That the pretender kills,
Receive your stumbling child
Drunk with the morning-dew
Into your fibrous love
With which creation's strung;
Embrace him, raise him high,
Keeping the old time young,
And hold him through the night
Our best hopes share, as bright,
As peerless as a cock's eye.

THE CLASS WILL COME TO ORDER

O tell me all about Anna Livia! I want to hear all about Anna Livia.
Well, you know Anna Livia? Yes, of course, we all know Anna Livia.
Tell me all. Tell me now. You'll die when you hear.

—Finnegans Wake

. . . ed io sorridendo li guardava, e nulla dicea loro.

—Vita Nuova

Amid that Platonic statuary, of athletes
Playing their passionate and sexless games,
The governors-to-be struck careless on the lawns,
The soldiers' monument, the sparrow-bronzes,
Through that museum of Corinthian elms
I walked among them in the
Soliloquy of summer, a gravel-scholar.

Our Irish friend had counseled silence first:
He did not mean the silence of the cowed,
But hold your tongue, sir, rather than betray.
Decorum is a face the brave can wear
In their desire to be invisible and so
To hear a music not prescribed, a tendril-tune
That climbs the porches of the ear,
Green, cool, like cucumber-vine.
What if the face starts threatening the man?
Then exile, cunning. Yes, old father, yes,
The newspapers were right,
Youth is general all over America,
The snow will not be falling till next winter,

124

There is no hurry yet to take my journey.
"The almonds bloom," she wrote. But will they hold,
While I remain to teach the alphabet
I still must learn, the alphabet on fire,
Those wizard stones? As always, where the text ends
Lurks the self, so shamed and magical. Away!
Who stays here long enough will stay too long.
Time snaps her fan, and there's her creature caught,
Fixed in the pleatings, fated to return
As thin as paper in the mother-folds.
Absurd though it may seem,
Perhaps there's too much order in this world;
The poets love to haul disorder in,
Braiding their wrists with her long mistress hair,
And when the house is tossed about our ears,
The governors must set it right again.
How wise was he who banned them from his state!

O tell me a tale before the lecture-bell!
I swear, Artificer, I swear I saw
Their souls awaiting me, with notebooks primed.
The lesson for today, the lessons what?
I must have known, but did not care to know.
There is a single theme, the heart declares,
That circumnavigates curriculum.
The letter in my pocket kissed my hand.
I smiled but I did not tell them,
I did not tell them why it was I smiled.

THE SUMMING-UP

When young I scribbled, boasting, on my wall,
No Love, No Property, No Wages.
In youth's good time I somehow bought them all,
And cheap, you'd think, for maybe a hundred pages.

Now in my prime, disburdened of my gear,
My trophies ransomed, broken, lost,
I carve again on the lintel of the year
My sign: MOBILITY—and damn the cost!

REVOLVING MEDITATION

How much I disapprove of it!
How little I love it!
Though, contrariwise,
Can there be
Anything half as dear?
God knows I've had my joys,
Tasted the honey on the branch
And picked a sprig or two
Of accidental laurel
Along the way;
But why do I wake at the sound,
In the middle of the night,
Of the tread of the Masked Man
Heavy on the stairs,
And from the street below
The lamentation of the wounded glove?
Agh! I am sometimes weary
Of this everlasting search
For the drama in a nutshell,
The opera of the tragic sense,
Which I would gladly be rid of.
A shameless keyhole god
Keeps spying on my worst,
Incontinently glued
To the obscene dumb show
Of the debasers of currency
In the private cabinet,
The dealers of soiled cards

At their desperate game . . .
And the double-dealers,
The ambiguous ones with their smeared
Faces, the acrobatic dancers—
Those who stood
Naked with me,
Adorable, adored,
On the magnet-head
Of the same inexorable pin.
Why should I be bothered with it?
Imagination cries
That in the grand accountancy
What happens to us is false;
Imagination makes,
Out of what stuff it can,
An action fit
For a more heroic stage
Than body ever walked on.
I have learned,
Trying to live
With this perjured quid of mine,
That the truth is not in the stones,
But in the architecture;
Equally, I am not deceived
By the triumph of the stuffing
Over the chair.
If I must build a church,
Though I do not really want one,
Let it be in the wilderness
Out of nothing but nail-holes.
I listen, I am always listening,

In fear that something might get by,
To the grammar of the public places,
But I fly toward Possibility,
In the extravagantly gay
Surprise of a journey,
Careless that I am bound
To the flaming wheel of my bones,
Preferring to hear, as I
Am forced to hear,
The voice of the solitary
Who makes others less alone,
The dialogue of lovers,
And the conversation of two worms
In the beam of a house,
Their mouths filled with sawdust.

A Spark of Laurel

This man, this poet, said,
"I've carried in my head
For twenty years and more
Some lines you wrote before
I knew the meaning of
Euripides or love"—
And gravely then intoned,
Lured from the underground
The greekness of my song
Still melancholy-young;
While she, long since forgotten,
For whom the song was written,
Burned wanton once again
Through centuries of rain,
Smiling, as she must do,
To keep her legend true,
And struck the mortal blow,
But not that blood could flow.
Ha! Once again I heard
The transubstantial word
That is not mine to speak
Unless I break, I break;
The spiral verb that weaves
Through the crystal of our lives,
Of myth and water made
And incoherent blood;
What sirens on the coast
Trilled to Ulysses lost,

And Agamemnon's thigh
Opened at length to cry:
This laurel-sparking rhyme
That we repeat in time
Until the fathers rest
On the inhuman breast
That is both fire and stone,
Mother and mistress, one.

THE TESTING-TREE

In a murderous time
the heart breaks and breaks
and lives by breaking.
It is necessary to go
through dark and deeper dark
and not to turn.
I am looking for the trail.
Where is my testing-tree?
Give me back my stones!

1971

Journal for My Daughter

1

Your turn. Grass of confusion.
You say you had a father once:
his name was absence.
He left, but did not let you go.
Part of him, more than a shadow,
beckoned down corridors,
secret, elusive, saturnine,
melting at your touch.
In the crack
of a divided house
grew the resentment-weed.
It has white inconspicuous flowers
Family of anthologists!
Collectors of injuries!

2

I wake to a glittering world,
to the annunciation of the frost.
A popeyed chipmunk scurries past,
the pockets of his cheeks bulging.
As the field mice store seeds,
as the needle-nosed shrew
threading under the woodpile
deposits little heaps of land-snails
for milestones on its runways,
I propose
that we gather our affections.
Lambkin, I care.

3

I was happy you were born,
your banks of digits
equipped for decimals,
and all your clever parts
neatly in place.
Your nation gives me joy,
as it has always given.
If I could have my choice
on the way to exile
I think I'd rather sleep forever
than wake up cold
in a country without women.

4

You cried. You cried.
You wasted and you cried.
Night after night
I walked the floor with you,
croaking the same old
tranquillizing song,
the only tune
I ever learned to carry.
In the rosy tissue
of your brain,
where memory begins,
that theme is surely scored,
waiting till you need
to play it back.
There were three crows
sat on a tree
Sing Billy Magee Magaw.

You do not need to sing to me.
I like the sound of your voice
even when you phone from school
asking for money.

5

There was a big blond uncle-bear,
wounded, smoke-eyed, wild,
who shambled from the west
with his bags full of havoc.
He spoke the bears' grunt-language,
waving his paws
and rocking on his legs.
Both of us were drunk,
slapping each other on the back,
sweaty with genius.
He spouted his nonsense-rhymes,
roaring like a behemoth.
You crawled under the sofa.

6

Goodies are shaken
from the papa-tree:
Be what you are. Give
what is yours to give.
Have style. Dare.
Such a storm of fortune cookies!
Outside your room
stands the white-headed prowler
in his multiple disguises
who reminds you of your likeness.

Wherever you turn,
down whatever street,
in the fugues of appetite,
in the groin of nightmare,
he waits for you,
haggard with his thousand years.
His agents are everywhere,
his heart is at home
in your own generation;
the folded message in his hands
is stiff with dirt and wine-stains,
older than the Dead Sea Scrolls.
Daughter, read:
What do I want of my life?
More! More!

7

Demonstrations in the streets.
I am there not there,
ever uneasy in a crowd.
But you belong,
flaunting your home-made
insubordinate flag.
Why should I be surprised?
We come of a flinty maverick line.
In my father's time, I'm told,
our table was set in turn
for Maxim Gorky, Emma Goldman,
and the atheist Ingersoll.
If your slogan is misspelt
Don't tred on me!
still it strikes

parents and politicians down.
Noli me tangere! is what
I used to cry in Latin once.
Oh to be radical, young, desirable, cool!

8

Your first dog was a Pekinese,
fat and saucy Ko-San,
half mandarin, half mini-lion,
who chased milkmen and mailmen
and bit the tires of every passing car
till a U.S. Royal bit him back.
You sobbed for half an hour,
then romped to the burial service
in the lower garden
by the ferny creek.
I helped you pick the stones
to mark his shallow grave.
It was the summer I went away.
One night I carried you outdoors,
in a blitz of fireflies,
to watch your first eclipse.
Your far-off voice,
drugged with milk and sleep,
said it was a leaf
sliding over the light.

9

The night when Coleridge,
heavy-hearted,
bore his crying child outside,

he noted
that those brimming eyes
caught the reflection
of the starry sky,
and each suspended tear
made a sparkling moon.

An Old Cracked Tune

My name is Solomon Levi,
the desert is my home,
my mother's breast was thorny,
and father I had none.

The sands whispered, *Be separate*,
the stones taught me, *Be hard*.
I dance, for the joy of surviving,
on the edge of the road.

The Portrait

My mother never forgave my father
for killing himself,
especially at such an awkward time
and in a public park,
that spring
when I was waiting to be born.
She locked his name
in her deepest cabinet
and would not let him out,
though I could hear him thumping.
When I came down from the attic
with the pastel portrait in my hand
of a long-lipped stranger
with a brave moustache
and deep brown level eyes,
she ripped it into shreds
without a single word
and slapped me hard.
In my sixty-fourth year
I can feel my cheek
still burning.

The Magic Curtain

At breakfast mother sipped her buttermilk,
    her mind already on her shop,
    unrolling gingham by the yard,
stitching her dresses for the Boston trade.
Behind her, Frieda with the yellow hair,
    capricious keeper of the toast,
    buckled her knees, as if she'd lost
balance and platter, then winked at me, blue-eyed.
Frieda, my first love! who sledded me to sleep
    through snows of the Bavarian woods
    into the bell-song of the girls,
with kinds of kisses mother would not dream;
tales of her wicked stepfather, a dwarf,
    from whom she fled to Bremerhaven
    with scarcely the tatters on her back;
riddles, nonsense, lieder, counting-songs. . . .
    Eins, zwei, drei, vier, fünf, sechs, sieben,
    Wo ist denn mein liebster Herr geblieben?
    Er ist nicht hier, er ist nicht da,
    Er ist fort nach Amerika.
"Be sure," said mother briskly at the door,
    "that you get Sonny off to school
    on time. And see that he combs his hair."
How could she guess what we two had in mind?

2

Downtown at the Front St. Bi-jo (spelt Bijou)
    we were, as always, the first in line,

with a hot nickel clutched in hand,
impatient for *The Perils of Pauline*,
my Frieda in her dainty blouse and skirt,
    I in my starched white sailor suit
    and buttoned shoes, prepared to hang
from cliffs, twist on a rack, be tied to rails.
School faded out at every morning reel,
    The Iron Claw held me in thrall,
    Cabiria taught me the Punic Wars,
at bloody Antietam I fought on Griffith's side.
And Keystone Kops came tumbling on the scene
    in outsized uniforms, moustached,
    their thick-browed faces dipped in flour,
to crank tin lizzies that immediately collapsed.
John Bunny held his belly when he laughed,
    ladies politely removed their hats,
    Cyrus of Persia stormed the gates,
upsetting our orgy at Belshazzar's Feast.
Then Charlie shuffled in on bunioned feet.
    We twirled with him an imaginary cane
    and blew our noses for the gallant poor
who bet on a horse, the horse that always loses.
Blanche Sweet, said Frieda, had a pretty name,
    but I came back with Arline Pretty,
    and, even sweeter, Louise Lovely.
Send me your picture, Violet Mersereau!
Lights up! Ushers with atomizers ranged
    the aisles, emitting lilac spray.
    We lunched on peanuts and Hershey bars
and moved to the Majestic for the two o'clock show.

3

Five . . . four . . . three . . . two . . . one . . .
     The frames are whirling backward, see!
     The operator's lost control.
Your story flickers on your bedroom wall.
Deaths, marriages, betrayals, lies,
     close-ups of tears, forbidden games,
     spill in a montage on a screen,
with chases, pratfalls, custard pies, and sores.
You have become your past, which time replays,
     to your surprise, as comedy.
     That coathanger neatly whisked your coat
right off your back. Soon it will want your skin.

     Five . . . four . . . three . . . two . . . one . . .
     Where has my dearest gone?
     She is nowhere to be found,
     She dwells in the underground.

Let the script revel in tricks and transformations.
     When the film is broken, let it be spliced
     where Frieda vanished one summer night
with somebody's husband, daddy to a brood.
And with her vanished, from the bureau drawer,
     the precious rose-enameled box
     that held those chestnut-colored curls
clipped from my sorrowing head when I was four.
After the war an unsigned picture-card
     from Dresden came, with one word: *Liebe*.
     "I'll never forgive her," mother said,
but as for me, I do and do and do.

AFTER THE LAST DYNASTY

Reading in Li Po
how "the peach blossom follows the water"
I keep thinking of you
because you were so much like
Chairman Mao,
naturally with the sex
transposed
and the figure slighter.
Loving you was a kind
of Chinese guerrilla war.
Thanks to your lightfoot genius
no Eighth Route Army
kept its lines more fluid,
traveled with less baggage,
so nibbled the advantage.
Even with your small bad heart
you made a dance of departures.
In the cold spring rains
when last you failed me
I had nothing left to spend
but a red crayon language
on the character of the enemy
to break appointments,
to fight us not
with his strength
but with his weakness,
to kill us
not with his health
but with his sickness.

Pet, spitfire, blue-eyed pony,
here is a new note
I want to pin on your door,
though I am ten years late
and you are nowhere:
Tell me,
are you still mistress of the valley,
what trophies drift downriver,
why did you keep me waiting?

THE ILLUMINATION

In that hotel my life
rolled in its socket
twisting my strings.
All my mistakes,
from my earliest
bedtimes,
rose against me:
the parent I denied,
the friends I failed,
the hearts I spoiled,
including at least
my own left ventricle—
a history of shame.
"Dante!" I cried
to the apparition
entering from the hall,
laureled and gaunt,
in a cone of light.
"Out of mercy you came
to be my Master
and my guide!"
To which he replied:
"I know neither the time
nor the way
nor the number on the door . . .
but this must be my room,
I was here before."
And he held up in his hand
the key,
which blinded me.

ROBIN REDBREAST

It was the dingiest bird
you ever saw, all the color
washed from him, as if
he had been standing in the rain,
friendless and stiff and cold,
since Eden went wrong.
In the house marked FOR SALE,
where nobody made a sound,
in the room where I lived
with an empty page, I had heard
the squawking of the jays
under the wild persimmons
tormenting him.
So I scooped him up
after they knocked him down,
in league with that ounce of heart
pounding in my palm,
that dumb beak gaping.
Poor thing! Poor foolish life!
without sense enough to stop
running in desperate circles,
needing my lucky help
to toss him back into his element.
But when I held him high,
fear clutched my hand,
for through the hole in his head,
cut whistle-clean . . .
through the old dried wound

between his eyes
where the hunter's brand
had tunneled out his wits . . .
I caught the cold flash of the blue
unappeasable sky.

River Road

That year of the cloud, when my marriage failed,
I slept in a chair, by the flagstone hearth,
fighting my sleep,
and one night saw a Hessian soldier
stand at attention there in full
regalia, till his head broke into flames.
My only other callers were the FBI
sent to investigate me as a Russian spy
by patriotic neighbors on the river road;
and flying squirrels parachuting from the elms
who squeaked in rodent heat between the walls
and upstairs rumbled at their nutty games.
I never dared open the attic door.
Even my nervous Leghorns joined the act,
indulging their taste for chicken from behind.
A glazed look swam into the survivors' eyes;
they caught a sort of dancing-sickness,
a variation of the blind staggers,
that hunched their narrow backs and struck
a stiffened wing akimbo,
as round and round the poultry yard
they flapped and dropped and flapped again.
The county agent shook his head:
not one of them was spared the cyanide.

That year of the cloud, when my marriage failed,
I paced up and down the bottom-fields,
tamping the mud-puddled nurslings in
with a sharp blow of the heel
timed to the chop-chop of the hoe:

red pine and white, larch, balsam fir,
one stride apart, two hundred to the row,
until I heard from Rossiter's woods
the downward spiral of a veery's song
unwinding on the eve of war.

Lord! Lord! who has lived so long?
Count it ten thousand trees ago,
five houses and ten thousand trees,
since the swallows exploded from Bowman Tower
over the place where the hermit sang,
while I held a fantail of squirming roots
that kissed the palm of my dirty hand,
as if in reply to a bird.
The stranger who hammers NO TRESPASS signs
to the staghorn sumac along the road
must think he owns this property.
I park my car below the curve
and climbing over the tumbled stones
where the wild foxgrape perseveres,
I walk into the woods I made,
my dark and resinous, blistered land,
through the deep litter of the years.

SUMMER SOLSTICE
—from Osip Mandelstam

Orioles live in the elms, and in classical verse
the length of the vowels alone determines the measure.
Once and once only a year nature knows quantity
stretched to the limit, as in Homer's meter.

O this is a day that yawns like a caesura:
serene from the start, almost painfully slowed.
Oxen browse in the field, and a golden languor
keeps me from drawing a rich, whole note from my reed.

TRISTIA

—from Osip Mandelstam

I made myself an expert in farewells
by studying laments, the nightfall of a woman's hair.
Oxen chew their cud; anticipation lags;
it is the town's last restless hour;
and I praise that ritual night when the cocks crowed
and eyelids, heavy with the griefs that pass,
opened to the light, while her weeping flowed
into the sound of the Muses singing.

Who knows, when the time comes to say good-bye,
what separation we are meant to bear
and what for us cockcrow shall signify
when the acropolis burns like a flare,
and why, at the new daybreak of a life,
when the ox is ruminating in his stall,
the herald cock, prophetic of rebirth,
should flap his wings on the town wall?

I bless the craft of spinning: the to-and-fro
action of the shuttle, the way the spindle hums.
Look! barefooted Delia, light as a feather,
hurries to meet you, flying as she comes.
Oh, how scrawny is the language of joy,
that weak foundation of our mortal lot!
Everything happened before; it will happen again.
Only the flash of recognition brings delight.
Be it so: a small transparent puppet lies,
like a dried squirrel-skin
extended on a plate,

while a girl crouches, staring, over the image.
Wax is for women what bronze is for men.
We, who move blindly toward a world of shades,
only in battle dare confront our fate;
but their gift is to die while telling fortunes.

THE MOUND BUILDERS

"Macon is the seventh layer of civilization on this spot."
—Ocmulgee National Monument, Georgia

I

Let the old geezers jig on Penn-
sylvania Avenue, and when the jig ends
let them offer a cracked tune
in praise of power:
the State counts the teeth of its friends.
All month, knee-deep in South,
oiled by Methodist money,
I have whirled to a different music
with oversweet, underdeveloped girls
who make me missionary.
My daughter sits in every class;
love is the tongue in my mouth.
Today through the streets of the Greek Revival
and the confederacy of the lawns
trumpeting with azaleas,
my rented Falcon flies
from the tiresome sound of my own voice,
the courteous chicken sitting on my plate,
and Sidney Lanier's exhausted flute
stuck in its cabinet of glass.
What's best in me lives underground,
rooting and digging, itching for wings;
my very worst imaginings
I give to the spoilers of the air.
At the National Park under a sky
of unshattered, unshatterable blue
I rejoice in the prevalence of green

and the starry chickweed of the fields.
Through the millennial ordeal
part, if only part of me, goes down
to the master farmers who built this mound,
this ceremonial earth-lodge,
and locked an eagle in it, shaped of clay,
the fork-eyed spotted bird of their cult,
and piled their dead in mounds higher and higher,
and raised up temple-mounds
to the giver of breath and corn
on which they stacked the harvest fire
that lit this stage for two hundred years.
Fifteen square miles! They must have known their power
stopped by the willows at the river's edge,
and yet it was too much to hold:
only their ghost-song haunts the field.

2

Musician of the lost tribes,
you summon to the council chamber,
to the elders in their scooped-out circle,
an earth-faced chorus of the lost,
people without name to remember,
led by stallion-proud Emperor Brim
bearing his feathered calumet,
chief of the tall Cowetas,
father of the Creek Nation,
by the Spaniards called "Gran Cazique,"
most feared redman of his generation;
foreshadowed, as a scroll unwinds,
by potters out of the swamps
who set their mark on the fanciful pipes they smoked

in the figure of birds or humans,
makers of bowls with carinated shoulders;
and their distant cousins, a patient cloud,
upholding jars with a smooth fold of the lip;
and, more dimly still, the shellfish eaters,
people of the stone axe,
who pitched their noisome camps
on their garbage heaps;
and straggling far behind,
out of primeval murk,
those wandering hunters in search of food
who crossed the land-bridge of the Bering Strait
and sliding over the glacier's edge
paved our first trails with their Mongol bones.
They followed the game that they pursued
into museums of prehistory,
featureless but for the fluted points
dropped from the bloodied mammoth's flanks.

3

The mounds rise up on every side
of a seven-layered world, as I stand
in the middle of the Ocmulgee fields,
by the Central of Georgia Railway track,
with the Creek braves under my feet
and the City of Macon at my back.

The Customs Collector's Report

For the sake of the record:
    on Tuesday, the 19th instant,
the third day of the storm,
    shortly before nightfall,
they swam over the pass together,
    this pair in their battered armor,
first seen in my spyglass;
    stovepipes assisting each other,
cylinders skating the snowcrust,
    comedians sprawling,
now and then dropping
    under the surface,
perceptible only
    as mounds in the driftage.

To whom, in this trial,
    could I turn for instructions?

At the north wall of the gorge,
    where zero poured to its funnel,
in the absence of guidelines
    I dared the encounter,
half-digging them out
    from the coils of the blizzard,
half-dying of cold
    as I scratched at the ice pack.
Then came issue of smothered voices,
    wind rumbling in empty barrels,
the sound of flags flapping
    in a cave of the mountain;

and the words that I heard
        flew by in tatters:
"nothing . . . nothing to declare . . .
        our wounds speak . . . heroes . . .
unfairly ambushed . . . the odds impossible . . .
        let our countrymen know . . . pride . . .
                honor . . .
how bravely . . . and oh
        what a body-count! . . ."
And the thinner voice cried,
        plaintively winding,
"True, brother, true! but tell me—
        what was the name of our war?"
When I lifted their helmets
        a gas escaped from them,
putrid, as from all battlefields,
        the last breath of the human.
That moment they were lightened.
        It seemed the earth shuddered,
the white tombs opened,
        disgorging their breastplates.
I saw them rise in the wind
        and roll off like ashcans.

Dear sirs, my lords, this
        is a lonely post:
all that I beg from you is your compassion.
        I petition you for transfer.

THE GLADIATORS

They fought in heavy armor
or, nimbly, with net and trident;
if lucky, against wild beasts,
but mostly against their brothers.

Criminals, captives, slaves,
what did they have to lose?
And the cheers egged them on,
as they waded through shit and blood.

When Claudius gave the sign
the throats of the fallen were cut
in the shade of the royal box:
he fancied their dying looks.

Domitian's coarser itch
was to set cripples on cripples.
No entertainment matched
the sport of their hacking and bleating.

Trajan's phantasmagoric show,
lasting a hundred days,
used up five thousand pairs
of jocks—and the count resumes.

A monk climbs out of the stands,
he is running onto the field,
he is waving his scrawny arms
to interrupt the games.

The mob tears him to bits.
Tomorrow the gates will be closed,
but the promised Crusades will start
with a torchlight children's parade.

THE SYSTEM

That pack of scoundrels
tumbling through the gate
emerges
as the Order of the State.

Around Pastor Bonhoeffer

THE PLOT AGAINST HITLER

Jittery, missing their cues,
Bach's glory jailed in their throats,
they were clustered round the piano
in the Biedermeier parlor,
sisters and brothers
and their brothers by marriage,
rehearsing a cantata
for Papa's seventy-fifth birthday.
Kyrie eleison: Night
like no other night, plotted
and palmed,
omega of terror,
packed like a bullet
in the triggered chamber.
Surely the men had arrived at their stations.
Through the staves of the music
he saw their target strutting,
baring its malignant heart.
Lord, let the phone ring!
Let the phone ring!

NEXT-TO-LAST THINGS

Slime, in the grain of the State,
like smut in the corn,
from the top infected.
Hatred made law,

wolves bred out of maggots
rolling in blood,
and the seal of the church ravished
to receive the crooked sign.
All the steeples were burning.
In the chapel of his ear
he had heard the midnight bells
jangling: *if you permit*
this evil, what is the good
of the good of your life?
And he forsook the last things,
the dear inviolable mysteries—
Plato's lamp, passed from the hand
of saint to saint—
that he might risk his soul in the streets,
where the things given
are only next to last;
in God's name cheating, pretending,
playing the double agent,
choosing to trade
the prayer for the deed,
and the deed most vile.
I am a liar and a traitor.

THE EXTERMINATION CAMP

Through the half-open door of the hut
the camp doctor saw him kneeling,
with his hands quietly folded.
"I was most deeply moved by the way
this lovable man prayed,
so devout and so certain

that God heard his prayer."
Round-faced, bespectacled, mild,
candid with costly grace,
he walked toward the gallows
and did not falter.
Oh but he knew the Hangman!
Only a few steps more
and he would enter the arcanum
where the Master
would take him by the shoulder,
as He does at each encounter,
and turn him round
to face his brothers in the world.

BOLSHEVIKS
—from Aba Stolzenberg

They came on ponies, barefoot,
brandishing guns that had no bullets;
wore ladies' hats backward; their leaders
with the look of deacons; and packs
of ox-men, heads wrapped in sacks.

They came in early autumn, shook down
the pears they could not pick by hand;
sprawled across sidewalks and church steps
and felt themselves masters of the land.

The motorcycles spring out of nowhere.
A blast from the roaring White Guards!
Of Trotsky's soldiers nothing remains here
but some sad little mounds near the woods.

THREE FLOORS

Mother was a crack of light
and a gray eye peeping;
I made believe by breathing hard
that I was sleeping.

Sister's doughboy on last leave
had robbed me of her hand;
downstairs at intervals she played
Warum on the baby grand.

Under the roof a wardrobe trunk
whose lock a boy could pick
contained a red Masonic hat
and a walking stick.

Bolt upright in my bed that night
I saw my father flying;
the wind was walking on my neck,
the windowpanes were crying.

THE FLIGHT OF APOLLO

1

Earth was my home, but even there I was a stranger. This
mineral crust. I walk like a swimmer. What titanic bom-
bardments in those old astral wars! I know what I know: I
shall never escape from strangeness or complete my journey.
Think of me as nostalgic, afraid, exalted. I am your man on
the moon, a speck of megalomania, restless for the leap to-
ward island universes pulsing beyond where the constella-
tions set. Infinite space overwhelms the human heart, but in
the middle of nowhere life inexorably calls to life. Forward
my mail to Mars. What news from the Great Spiral Nebula
in Andromeda and the Magellanic Clouds?

2

I was a stranger on earth.
Stepping on the moon, I begin
the gay pilgrimage to new
Jerusalems
in foreign galaxies.
Heat. Cold. Craters of silence.
The Sea of Tranquility
rolling on the shores of entropy.
And, beyond,
the intelligence of the stars.

KING OF THE RIVER

If the water were clear enough,
if the water were still,
but the water is not clear,
the water is not still,
you would see yourself,
slipped out of your skin,
nosing upstream,
slapping, thrashing,
tumbling
over the rocks
till you paint them
with your belly's blood:
Finned Ego,
yard of muscle that coils,
uncoils.

If the knowledge were given you,
but it is not given,
for the membrane is clouded
with self-deceptions
and the iridescent image swims
through a mirror that flows,
you would surprise yourself
in that other flesh
heavy with milt,
bruised, battering toward the dam
that lips the orgiastic pool.

Come. Bathe in these waters.
Increase and die.

If the power were granted you
to break out of your cells,
but the imagination fails
and the doors of the senses close
on the child within,
you would dare to be changed,
as you are changing now,
into the shape you dread
beyond the merely human.
A dry fire eats you.
Fat drips from your bones.
The flutes of your gills discolor.
You have become a ship for parasites.
The great clock of your life
is slowing down,
and the small clocks run wild.
For this you were born.
You have cried to the wind
and heard the wind's reply:
"I did not choose the way,
the way chose me."
You have tasted the fire on your tongue
till it is swollen black
with a prophetic joy:
"Burn with me!
The only music is time,
the only dance is love."

If the heart were pure enough,
but it is not pure,
you would admit
that nothing compels you
any more, nothing

at all abides,
but nostalgia and desire,
the two-way ladder
between heaven and hell.
On the threshold
of the last mystery,
at the brute absolute hour,
you have looked into the eyes
of your creature self,
which are glazed with madness,
and you say
he is not broken but endures,
limber and firm
in the state of his shining,
forever inheriting his salt kingdom,
from which he is banished
forever.

THE MULCH

A man with a leaf in his head
watches an indefatigable gull
dropping a piss-clam on the rocks
to break it open.
Repeat. Repeat.
He is an inlander
who loves the margins of the sea,
and everywhere he goes he carries
a bag of earth on his back.
Why is he down in the tide marsh?
Why is he gathering salt hay
in bushel baskets crammed to his chin?
"It is a blue and northern air,"
he says, as if the shiftings of the sky
had taught him husbandry.
Birthdays for him are when he wakes
and falls into the news of weather.
"Try! Try!" clicks the beetle in his wrist,
his heart is an educated swamp,
and he is mindful of his garden,
which prepares to die.

INDIAN SUMMER AT LAND'S END

The season stalls, unseasonably fair,
blue-fair, serene, a stack of golden discs,
each disc a day, and the addition slow.
I wish you were here with me to walk the flats,
toward dusk especially when the tide is out
and the bay turns opal, filled with rolling fire
that washes on the mouldering wreck offshore,
our mussel-vineyard, strung with bearded grapes.
Last night I reached for you and shaped you there
lying beside me as we drifted past
the farthest seamarks and the watchdog bells,
and round Long Point throbbing its frosty light,
until we streamed into the open sea.
What did I know of voyaging till now?
Meanwhile I tend my flock, small golden puffs
impertinent as wrens, with snipped-off tails,
who bounce down from the trees. High overhead,
on the trackless roads, skywriting V and yet
another V, the southbound Canada express
hoots of horizons and distances. . . .

CLEOPATRA

—from Anna Akhmatova

She had already kissed Antony's dead lips,
she had already wept on her knees before Caesar . . .
and her servants have betrayed her. Darkness falls.
The trumpets of the Roman eagle scream.

And in comes the last man to be ravished by her beauty—
such a tall gallant!—with a shamefaced whisper:
"You must walk before him, as a slave, in the triumph."
But the slope of her swan's neck is tranquil as ever.

Tomorrow they'll put her children in chains. Nothing
remains except to tease this fellow out of mind
and put the black snake, like a parting act of pity,
on her dark breast with indifferent hand.

DANTE

—from Anna Akhmatova

Even after his death he did not return
to the city that nursed him.
Going away, this man did not look back.
To him I sing this song.
Torches, night, a last embrace,
outside in her streets the mob howling.
He sent her a curse from hell
and in heaven could not forget her.
But never, in a penitent's shirt,
did he walk barefoot with lighted candle
through his beloved Florence,
perfidious, base, and irremediably home.

BORIS PASTERNAK

—from Anna Akhmatova

He who has compared himself to the eye of a horse
peers, looks, sees, identifies,
and instantly like molten diamonds
puddles shine, ice grieves and liquefies.

In lilac mists the backyards drowse,
and depots, logs, leaves, clouds above;
that hooting train, that crunch of watermelon rind,
that timid hand in a perfumed kid glove . . .

All's ringing, roaring, grinding, breakers' crash—
and silence all at once, release;
it means he is tiptoeing over pine needles,
so as not to startle the light sleep of space.

And it means he is counting the grains
in the blasted ears; it means
he has come again to the Daryal Gorge,
accursed and black, from another funeral.

And again Moscow, where the heart's fever burns;
far off the deadly sleighbell chimes;
someone is lost two steps from home
in waist-high snow. The worst of times . . .

For spying Laocoön in a puff of smoke,
for making a song out of graveyard thistles,
for filling the world with a new sound
of verse reverberating in new space,

he has been rewarded by a kind of eternal childhood,
with the generosity and brilliance of the stars;
the whole of the earth was his to inherit,
and his to share with every human spirit.

THE ARTIST

His paintings grew darker every year.
They filled the walls, they filled the room;
eventually they filled his world—
all but the ravishment.
When voices faded, he would rush to hear
the scratched soul of Mozart
endlessly in gyre.
Back and forth, back and forth,
he paced the paint-smeared floor,
diminishing in size each time he turned,
trapped in his monumental void,
raving against his adversaries.
At last he took a knife in his hand
and slashed an exit for himself
between the frames of his tall scenery.
Through the holes of his tattered universe
the first innocence and the light
came pouring in.

THE TESTING-TREE

I

On my way home from school
    up tribal Providence Hill
        past the Academy ballpark
where I could never hope to play
    I scuffed in the drainage ditch
        among the sodden seethe of leaves
hunting for perfect stones
    rolled out of glacial time
        into my pitcher's hand;
then sprinted lickety-
    split on my magic Keds
        from a crouching start,
scarcely touching the ground
    with my flying skin
        as I poured it on
for the prize of the mastery
    over that stretch of road,
        with no one no where to deny
when I flung myself down
    that on the given course
        I was the world's fastest human.

2

Around the bend
    that tried to loop me home
        dawdling came natural

across a nettled field
       riddled with rabbit-life
              where the bees sank sugar-wells
in the trunks of the maples
       and a stringy old lilac
              more than two stories tall
blazing with mildew
       remembered a door in the
              long teeth of the woods.
All of it happened slow:
       brushing the stickseed off,
              wading through jewelweed
strangled by angel's hair,
       spotting the print of the deer
              and the red fox's scats.

Once I owned the key
       to an umbrageous trail
              thickened with mosses
where flickering presences
       gave me right of passage
              as I followed in the steps
of straight-backed Massassoit
       soundlessly heel-and-toe
              practicing my Indian walk.

       3
Past the abandoned quarry
       where the pale sun bobbed
              in the sump of the granite,
past copperhead ledge,
       where the ferns gave foothold,
              I walked, deliberate,

on to the clearing,
      with the stones in my pocket
         changing to oracles
and my coiled ear turned
      to the slightest leaf-stir.
         I had kept my appointment.
There I stood in the shadow,
      at fifty measured paces,
         of the inexhaustible oak,
tyrant and target,
      Jehovah of acorns,
         watchtower of the thunders,
that locked King Philip's War
      in its annulated core
         under the cut of my name.
Father wherever you are
      I have only three throws
         bless my good right arm.
In the haze of afternoon,
      while the air flowed saffron,
         I played my game for keeps—
for love, for poetry,
      and for eternal life—
         after the trials of summer.

    4

In the recurring dream
      my mother stands
         in her bridal gown
under the burning lilac,
      with Bernard Shaw and Bertie
         Russell kissing her hands;

the house behind her is in ruins;
      she is wearing an owl's face
         and makes barking noises.
Her minatory finger points.
      I pass through the cardboard doorway
         askew in the field
and peer down a well
      where an albino walrus huffs.
         He has the gentlest eyes.
If the dirt keeps sifting in,
      staining the water yellow,
         why should I be blamed?
Never try to explain.
      That single Model A
         sputtering up the grade
unfurled a highway behind
      where the tanks maneuver,
         revolving their turrets.
In a murderous time
      the heart breaks and breaks
         and lives by breaking.
It is necessary to go
      through dark and deeper dark
         and not to turn.
I am looking for the trail.
      Where is my testing-tree?
         Give me back my stones!

THE GAME

Let's spin the bottle
No I don't want to be kissed

Sometimes I feel my arm
Is turning into a tree

Or hardening to stone
Past memory of green

I've a long way to go
Who never learned to pray

O the night is coming on
And I am nobody's son

Father it's true
But only for a day.

FROM

THE LAYERS

I have walked through many lives,
some of them my own,
and I am not who I was,
though some principle of being
abides, from which I struggle
not to stray.

IN
THE POEMS OF STANLEY KUNITZ
1928–1978

THE KNOT

I've tried to seal it in,
that cross-grained knot
on the opposite wall,
scored in the lintel of my door,
but it keeps bleeding through
into the world we share.
Mornings when I wake,
curled in my web,
I hear it come
with a rush of resin
out of the trauma
of its lopping-off.
Obstinate bud,
sticky with life,
mad for the rain again,
it racks itself with shoots
that crackle overhead,
dividing as they grow.
Let be! Let be!
I shake my wings
and fly into its boughs.

WHAT OF THE NIGHT?

1

One summer, like a stone
dropped down a well,
I sank into myself
and raked
the bottom slime.
When I stretched out my thigh
it touched the dark,
and the dark rolled over me.
A brackish life
filled the cups of my skin.
Then gradually I heard
above the steady
breathing of the land
a high, inhuman chord
light-years away,
out of a cleaner space,
a more innocent age,
as when pilot angels
with crystal eyes and streaming hair
rode planets through the skies,
and each one sang
a single ravishing note
that melted
into the music of the spheres.

2

What wakes me now
like the country doctor
startled in his sleep?

Why does my racing heart
shuffle down the hall
for the hundredth time
to answer the night-bell?
Whoever summons me has need of me.
How could I afford
to disobey that call?
A gentle, insistent ring
pulled me from my bed,
from loving arms,
though I know
I am not ready yet
and nobody stands on the stoop,
not even a stray cat
slouches under the sodium lamp.
Deceived! or self-deceived.
I can never atone for it.
Oh I should be the one
to swell the night with my alarm!
When the messenger comes again
I shall pretend
in a childish voice
my father is not home.

QUINNAPOXET

I was fishing in the abandoned reservoir
back in Quinnapoxet,
where the snapping turtles cruised
and the bullheads swayed
in their bower of tree-stumps,
sleek as eels and pigeon-fat.
One of them gashed my thumb
with a flick of his razor fin
when I yanked the barb
out of his gullet.
The sun hung its terrible coals
over Buteau's farm: I saw
the treetops seething.

They came suddenly into view
on the Indian road,
evenly stepping
past the apple orchard,
commingling with the dust
they raised, their cloud of being,
against the dripping light
looming larger and bolder.
She was wearing a mourning bonnet
and a wrap of shining taffeta.
"Why don't you write?" she cried
from the folds of her veil.
"We never hear from you."
I had nothing to say to her.
But for him who walked behind her
in his dark worsted suit,

with his face averted
as if to hide a scald,
deep in his other life,
I touched my forehead
with my swollen thumb
and splayed my fingers out—
in deaf-mute country
the sign for father.

Words for the Unknown Makers
*A Garland of Commemorative Verses**

TO A SLAVE NAMED JOB

Dreaming of Africa
and the kings of the dark land,
bearer of a suffering name,
you carved this Indian
out of a man-sized log
to be your surrogate
and avatar.
Outside the smoke-shop
he stands aloof and bold,
with his raised foot poised
for the oppressor's neck.
The cigars he offers
are not for sale.
They fit his hand
as though they were a gun.

SACRED TO THE MEMORY

Mourn for Polly Botsford, aged thirty-nine,
and for her blossom Polly, one year old,
and for Gideon, her infant son, nipped in the bud.
And mourn for the mourners under the graveside willow,
trailing its branches of inverted V's, those women

*On the occasion of the exhibition "The Flowering of American Folk Art," at the
Whitney Museum in 1974. See Note on p. 273.

propped like bookends on either side of the tomb,
and that brace of innocents in matching calico
linked to their mother's grief with a zigzag clasp of hands,
as proper in their place as stepping-stones.
Mourn, too, for the nameless painter of the scene
who, like them all, was born to walk a while
beside the brook whose source is common tears,
till suddenly it's time to unlatch the narrow gate
and pass through the church that is not made with walls
and seek another home, a different sky.

GIRL WITH SAMPLER
"A Soft Answer Turneth Away Wrath"

She sat by the window,
lips pursed, plying her needle.
The parlor wall waited
for a family showpiece.
"Do it right, child!" said her mother.
This way she learned the ABC's,
improved her mind with Bible verses,
embroidered her name into her dowry:
Nabby Dexter of Providence, Rhode Island,
Patricia Goodeshall, Abigail Fleetwood,
Elizabeth Finney, virtuoso of stitches
(cross . . . flat . . . buttonhole . . .
satin . . . outline . . . bullion knot).
Some prized the task and its performance,
others groaned as they ripped out blunders
in and around the moral sentences.
One of them added a line to her sampler:
"And Hated every bit of it."

TROMPE L'OEIL

Whoever made this piece began
with boards of honest country pine
fit for a modest sideboard table.
As for finishing,
I doubt he had a plan,
he simply led his brushes on,
or maybe it was they that led,
stippling and graining,
simulating to a T
maple, walnut, birch,
imitating inlays and veneers,
putting on the airs of Sheraton.
Utility took fantasy for wife.
O lucky day!
The fun was in the afterplay
when the true artisan
tells his white lies.

A BLESSING OF WOMEN

> *"Remember me is all I ask,*
> *And, if remembered be a task,*
> *Forget me."*
>
> —Album verses by Minerva Butler Miller,
> tinsmith's daughter, peddler's wife, C. 1850

BLESS ZERUAH HIGLEY GUERNSEY of Castleton, Vermont,
who sheared the wool from her father's sheep; washed,
carded, and spun it into yarn; steeped it in dyes concocted

from native berries, barks, and plants; and embroidered it, in Double Kensington chain stitch, on a ground of homespun squares until they bloomed with fruit, shells, snow crystals, flowers, and cats, most singularly a noble blue cat; each of the eighty-odd panels being different from the rest, and the whole a paragon of American needlework design, executed in the ardor of her long pre-nuptial flight, and accomplished in 1835 for her ill-starred wedding day.

BLESS DEBORAH GOLDSMITH, genteel itinerant, who supported her aged and impoverished parents by traveling from house to house in the environs of Hamilton, New York, painting portraits of the families who gave her bed and board, until she limned in watercolors the likeness of one George Throop, who married her, therewith terminating her travels and leading to her premature decease, at twenty-seven.

BLESS MRS. AUSTIN ERNEST of Paris, Illinois, whose husband, a local politician of no other fame, organized in 1853 a rally for the Presidential candidate of the new Republican party, following which she gathered the material used to decorate the stand wherefrom the immortal Lincoln spoke and, with scissors and needle and reverential heart, transformed it into a quilted patchwork treasure.

BLESS MARY ANN WILLSON, who in 1810 appeared in the frontier town of Greenville, New York, with her "romantic attachment," a Miss Brundage, with whom she settled in a log cabin, sharing their lives and their gifts, Miss Brundage farming the land, Miss Willson painting dramatic scenes with a bold hand, in colors derived from berries, brickdust, and store paint, and offering her compositions for sale as "rare and unique works of art."

BLESS HANNAH COHOON, who dwelt in the Shaker "City of Peace," Hancock, Massachusetts, where a spirit visited her, as frequently happened there, and gave her "a draft of a beautiful Tree pencil'd on a large sheet of white paper," which she copied out, not knowing till later, with assistance from the Beyond, that it was the Tree of Life; and who saw in another vision, which she likewise reproduced, the Elders of the community feasting on cakes at a table beneath mulberry trees; and who believed, according to the faith of the followers of Mother Ann Lee, that Christ would return to earth in female form.

BLESS IN A CONGREGATION, because they are so numerous, those industrious schoolgirls stitching their alphabets; and the deft ones with needles at lacework, crewel, knitting; and mistresses of spinning, weaving, dyeing; and daughters of tinsmiths painting their ornamental mottoes; and hoarders of rags hooking and braiding their rugs; and adepts in cutouts, valentines, stencils, still lifes, and "fancy pieces"; and middleaged housewives painting, for the joy of it, landscapes and portraits; and makers of bedcovers with names that sing in the night—Rose of Sharon, Princess Feather, Delectable Mountains, Turkey Tracks, Drunkard's Path, Indiana Puzzle, Broken Dishes, Star of LeMoyne, Currants and Coxcomb, Rocky-Road-to-Kansas.

BLESS THEM AND GREET THEM as they pass from their long obscurity, through the gate that separates us from our history, a moving rainbow-cloud of witnesses in a rising hubbub, jubilantly turning to greet one another, this tumult of sisters.

196

THE CATCH

It darted across the pond
toward our sunset perch,
weaving in, up, and around
a spindle of air,
this delicate engine
fired by impulse and glitter,
swift darning-needle,
gossamer dragon,
less image than thought,
and the thought come alive.
Swoosh went the net
with a practiced hand.
"Da-da, may I look too?"
You may look, child,
all you want.
This prize belongs to no one.
But you will pay all
your life for the privilege,
all your life.

THE CRYSTAL CAGE

for Joseph Cornell

To climb the belltower,
step after step,
in the grainy light,
without breathing harder;
to spy on each landing
a basket of gifts,
a snowbox of wonders:
pressed flowers, pieces
of colored glass,
a postcard from Niagara Falls,
agates, cut-outs of birds,
and dozing in the pile,
in faded mezzotint,
Child Mozart at the Clavichord.
Three days you fasted
to bring you angels;
your square-toed shoes,
friends of your plodding,
are turning weightless.
When the pear-shaped, brindled cat
who lives under the belfry
jumps into your arms
you are not surprised
by the love-look in her amber eyes,
or by the blissful secrets
she confides to you
in oval, pellucid tones.

What if the iron overhead
suddenly starts pounding?
What if, outside,
a terrible storm is raging?
What if, below,
your twisted brother is calling?

Signs and Portents

I

Jonathan, the last of the giant tortoises
on wind-beaten Saint Helena,
misses his island mate,
who died in a fall from a cliff
a century ago.
He is ancient and crusty,
more lonely than Bonaparte
strutting on the volcanic beach,
reviewing his triumphs.
Lately he has made himself
a deliberate nuisance
to the sporting set
of the British Crown Colony
by butting and upending benches
near the tennis courts
and disrupting croquet games
by sitting on the croquet balls.

2

At the Porch of the Caryatids
on the Acropolis
the noble supportive maidens
are stepping down
from their weathered pedestals,
one by one,
to seek asylum in a museum.
Their places will be taken
by identical synthetic sisters

conditioned to withstand
the high, classic, polluted air.

3

Three thousand years ago
they soaked him in pickling brine,
stuffed his body with resins,
baked him in desert heat.
He was Ramses the Second,
feared by Hittites and Israelites,
the hard Pharaoh of Exodus,
colossal as the temples
his minions sweated out of rock.
Paris has him now
on temporary loan.
In the aseptic laboratory
of the Musée de l'Homme,
where he lies in state
for special treatment,
who will cure the old mummy
of the loathsome fire
raging under his bandages?

4

Children at play in a field,
tumbling down a hole
into the pristine Palaeolithic,
showed us the way,
ripped the lid from the grotto.
We sped to the spot on wheels
with our cameras and basket lunches.

Now the bison of Lascaux,
prodded from their centuries
of limestone sleep, are sick.
Clots of a virulent mold
suppurate on their flanks,
emitting a green stain.
We name it *la maladie verte*,
an infection from people.
At the back of our minds
squat figures, whose hairy hands
carried torches and the dream of art
through cheerless labyrinths,
gabble in the shadows.

5

On Twelfth Street in Manhattan,
opposite St. Vincent's Mental Pavilion,
while I was sweeping the sidewalk
of its increment of filth,
deposited by dogs and unleashed humans,
a blue van rolled by
with its sidepanel reading;
WORLD FINISHING AND DYEING COMPANY.
I did not catch the face of the driver.

FIRESTICKS

Conjugations of the verb "to be"
asleep since Adam's fall
wake from bad phosphor dreams
heavy with mineral desire.
Earthstruck they leave
their ferny prints of spines
in beds of stone
and carry private moons
down history's long roads,
gaudy with flags.
The one they walk behind
who's named "I AM"
they chose with spurts of flame
to guide them
like the pillar of a cloud
into the mind's white exile.

THE LINCOLN RELICS

"*A Lincoln exhibit on view in the Great Hall makes the
16th President of the United States, born 167 years ago,
seem very real. Displayed are the contents of his pockets
the night he was assassinated, a miniature portrait never
before exhibited, and two great documents from the Li-
brary's collections, the Gettysburg Address and the Sec-
ond Inaugural Address.*"
             —February 1976,
                   Library of Congress Information Bulletin

I

Cold-eyed, in Naples once,
while the congregation swooned,
I watched the liquefaction
of a vial of precious blood,
and wondered only
how the trick was done.
Saint's bones are only bones
to me, but here,
where the stage is set
without a trace of gore,
these relics on display—
watchfob and ivory pocket knife,
a handkerchief of Irish linen,
a button severed from his sleeve—
make a noble, dissolving music
out of homely fife and drum,
and that's miraculous.

2

His innocence was to trust
the better angels of our nature,
even when the Union cracked
and furious blood
ran north and south
along the lines of pillage.
Secession grieved him
like the falling-out of brothers.
After Appomattox he laid
the white flower of forgiving
on Lee's crisp sword.
What was there left for him to do?
When the curtain rose
on *Our American Cousin*
he leaned forward in his chair
toward the last absurdity,
that other laughable country,
for which he was ready with his ransom—
a five-dollar Confederate note
in mint condition, and nine
newspaper accolades
neatly folded in his wallet.
It was time for him now
to try on his gold-rimmed spectacles,
the pair with the sliding temples
mended with a loop of string,
while the demon of the absolute,
who had been skulking in the wings,
leaped into focus,
waving a smoking pistol.

3

In the Great Hall of the Library,
as in a glass aquarium,
Abe Lincoln is swimming around,
dressed to the nines
in his stovepipe hat
and swallow-tailed coat,
effortlessly swimming,
propelled by sudden little kicks
of his gunboat shoes.
His billowing pockets hang
inside out; he is swimming
around, lighter at each turn,
giddy with loss,
while his memory sifts
to the sticky floor.
He is slipping away from us
into his legend and his fame,
having relinquished, piece by piece,
what he carried next to his skin,
what rocked to his angular stride,
partook of his man-smell,
shared the intimacy of his needs.
Mr. President,
in this Imperial City,
awash in gossip and power,
where marble eats marble
and your office has been defiled,
I saw the piranhas darting
between the rose-veined columns,
avid to strip the flesh
from the Republic's bones.
Has no one told you

how the slow blood leaks
from your secret wound?

    4

To be old and to be young
again, inglorious private
in the kitchens of the war
that winter of blackout,
walking by the Potomac
in melancholy khaki,
searching for the prairie star,
westward scanning the horizon
for its eloquent and magnanimous light,
yearning to be touched by its fire:
to be touched again, with the years
swirling at my feet, faces
blowing in the wind
around me where I stand,
withered, in the Great Hall.

    5

He steps out from the crowd
with his rawboned, warty look,
a gangling fellow in jeans
next to a plum-colored sari,
and just as suddenly he's gone.
But there's that other one
who's tall and lonely.

MEDITATIONS ON DEATH

—*from Giuseppe Ungaretti*

I

O sister of the shadow,
blackest in strongest light,
Death, you pursue me.

In a pure garden
innocent desire conceived you
and peace was lost,
pensive death,
on your mouth.

From that moment
I hear you in the mind's flow,
sounding the far depths,
suffering rival of eternity.

Poisonous mother of the ages,
fearful of palpitation
and of solitude,

beauty punished and smiling,
in the drowse of flesh
runaway dreamer,
unsleeping athlete
of our greatness,

when you have tamed me, tell me:
in the melancholy of the living
how long will my shadow fly?

II

Probing the deepest selves
of our unhappy mask
(enclosure of the infinite)
with fanatic blandishment—
the dark vigil of our fathers.

Death, mute word,
riverbed of sand deposited
by the blood,
I hear you singing like a locust
in the darkened rose of reflections.

III

Etcher of the secret wrinkles
in our unhappy mask—
the infinite jest of our fathers.

You, in the deep light,
O confused silence,
insist like the angry locusts.

IV

Clouds took me by the hand.

On the hillside I burn space and time,
like one of your messengers,
like a dream, divine death.

V

You have closed your eyes.

A night is born
full of hidden wounds,

of dead sounds
as of corks
when the nets are let down to the water.

Your hands become a breath
of inviolable distances,
slippery as thoughts,

And that equivocation of the moon
and that gentlest rocking,
if you would lay them on my eyes,
touch the soul.

You are the woman who passes by
like a leaf

leaving an autumn fire in the trees.

VI

O beautiful prey,
night-voice,
your movements
breed a fever.

Only you, demented memory,
could capture freedom.

On your elusive flesh
trembling in clouded mirrors
what crimes, I wonder,
did you not teach me to consummate?

With you, phantoms, I have no reticences,

and my heart is filled with your remorse
when it is day.

The Quarrel

The word I spoke in anger
weighs less than a parsley seed,
but a road runs through it
that leads to my grave,
that bought-and-paid-for lot
on a salt-sprayed hill in Truro
where the scrub pines
overlook the bay.
Half-way I'm dead enough,
strayed from my own nature
and my fierce hold on life.
If I could cry, I'd cry,
but I'm too old to be
anybody's child.
Liebchen,
with whom should I quarrel
except in the hiss of love,
that harsh, irregular flame?

THE UNQUIET ONES

Years ago I lost
both my parents' addresses.
Father and mother lie
in their neglected cribs,
obscure as moles,
unvisited.
I do not need to summon them.
When I put out the light
I hear them stir, dissatisfied,
in their separate places,
in death as in life
remote from each other,
having no conversation
except in the common ground
of their son's mind.
They slip through narrow crevices
and, suddenly blown tall,
glide into my cave of phantoms,
unwelcome guests, but not
unloved, dark emissaries
of the two-faced god.

My Sisters

Who whispered, souls have shapes?
So has the wind, I say.
But I don't know,
I only feel things blow.

I had two sisters once
with long black hair
who walked apart from me
and wrote the history of tears.
Their story's faded with their names,
but the candlelight they carried,
like dancers in a dream,
still flickers on their gowns
as they bend over me
to comfort my night-fears.

Let nothing grieve you,
Sarah and Sophia.
Shush, shush, my dears,
now and forever.

ROUTE SIX

The city squats on my back.
I am heart-sore, stiff-necked,
exasperated. That's why
I slammed the door,
that's why I tell you now,
in every house of marriage
there's room for an interpreter.
Let's jump into the car, honey,
and head straight for the Cape,
where the cock on our housetop crows
that the weather's fair,
and my garden waits for me
to coax it into bloom.
As for those passions left
that flare past understanding,
like bundles of dead letters
out of our previous lives
that amaze us with their fevers,
we can stow them in the rear
along with ziggurats of luggage
and Celia, our transcendental cat,
past-mistress of all languages,
including Hottentot and silence.
We'll drive non-stop till dawn,
and if I grow sleepy at the wheel,
you'll keep me awake by singing
in your bravura Chicago style
Ruth Etting's smoky song,

"Love Me or Leave Me,"
belting out the choices.

Light glazes the eastern sky
over Buzzards Bay.
Celia gyrates upward
like a performing seal,
her glistening nostrils aquiver
to sniff the brine-spiked air.
The last stretch toward home!
Twenty summers roll by.

THE LAYERS

I have walked through many lives,
some of them my own,
and I am not who I was,
though some principle of being
abides, from which I struggle
not to stray.
When I look behind,
as I am compelled to look
before I can gather strength
to proceed on my journey,
I see the milestones dwindling
toward the horizon
and the slow fires trailing
from the abandoned camp-sites,
over which scavenger angels
wheel on heavy wings.
Oh, I have made myself a tribe
out of my true affections,
and my tribe is scattered!
How shall the heart be reconciled
to its feast of losses?
In a rising wind
the manic dust of my friends,
those who fell along the way,
bitterly stings my face.
Yet I turn, I turn,
exulting somewhat,
with my will intact to go
wherever I need to go,

and every stone on the road
precious to me.
In my darkest night,
when the moon was covered
and I roamed through wreckage,
a nimbus-clouded voice
directed me:
"Live in the layers,
not on the litter."
Though I lack the art
to decipher it,
no doubt the next chapter
in my book of transformations
is already written.
I am not done with my changes.

NEXT-TO-LAST THINGS

Peace! Peace!
To be rocked by the Infinite!
As if it didn't matter
which way was home;
as if he didn't know
he loved the earth so much
he wanted to stay forever.

1985

THE SNAKES OF SEPTEMBER

All summer I heard them
rustling in the shrubbery,
outracing me from tier
to tier in my garden,
a whisper among the viburnums,
a signal flashed from the hedgerow,
a shadow pulsing
in the barberry thicket.
Now that the nights are chill
and the annuals spent,
I should have thought them gone,
in a torpor of blood
slipped to the nether world
before the sickle frost.
Not so. In the deceptive balm
of noon, as if defiant of the curse
that spoiled another garden,
these two appear on show
through a narrow slit
in the dense green brocade
of a north-country spruce,
dangling head-down, entwined
in a brazen love-knot.
I put out my hand and stroke
the fine, dry grit of their skins.
After all,
we are partners in this land,
co-signers of a covenant.
At my touch the wild
braid of creation
trembles.

THE ABDUCTION

Some things I do not profess
to understand, perhaps
not wanting to, including
whatever it was they did
with you or you with them
that timeless summer day
when you stumbled out of the wood,
distracted, with your white blouse torn
and a bloodstain on your skirt.
"Do you believe?" you asked.
Between us, through the years,
from bits, from broken clues,
we pieced enough together
to make the story real:
how you encountered on the path
a pack of sleek, grey hounds,
trailed by a dumbshow retinue
in leather shrouds; and how
you were led, through leafy ways,
into the presence of a royal stag,
flaming in his chestnut coat,
who kneeled on a swale of moss
before you; and how you were borne
aloft in triumph through the green,
stretched on his rack of budding horn,
till suddenly you found yourself alone
in a trampled clearing.

That was a long time ago,
almost another age, but even now,
when I hold you in my arms,
I wonder where you are.
Sometimes I wake to hear
the engines of the night thrumming
outside the east bay window
on the lawn spreading to the rose garden.
You lie beside me in elegant repose,
a hint of transport hovering on your lips,
indifferent to the harsh green flares
that swivel through the room,
searchlights controlled by unseen hands.
Out there is childhood country,
bleached faces peering in
with coals for eyes.
Our lives are spinning out
from world to world;
the shapes of things
are shifting in the wind.
What do we know
beyond the rapture and the dread?

Raccoon Journal

JULY 14

rac-coon', n. from the American Indian (Algonquian)
arahkunem, "he scratches with the hands."
                                    —*New World Dictionary*

JULY 17

They live promiscuously in the woods
above the marsh, snuggling in hollow trees
or rock-piled hillside dens,
from which they swagger in dead of night,
nosy, precocious, bushy-tailed,
to inspect their properties in town.

At every house they drop a calling card,
doorstep deposits of soft reddish scats
and heavy sprays of territorial scent
that on damp mornings mixes with the dew.

AUGUST 21–26

I've seen them, under the streetlight,
paddling up the lane,
five pelts in single file,
halting in unison to topple
a garbage can and gorge
on lobster shells and fish heads

or scattered parts of chicken.
Last year my neighbor's dog,
a full-grown Labrador retriever,
chased a grizzly old codger
into the tidal basin,
where shaggy arms reached up
from the ooze to embrace him,
dragging his muzzle under
until at length he drowned.

There's nobody left this side
of Gull Hill to tangle
with them, certainly not
my superannuated cat,
domesticated out of nature,
who stretches by the stove
and puts on a show of bristling.
She does that even when mice
go racing round the kitchen.
We seem to be two of a kind,
though that's not to say I'm happy
paying my vegetable tithe
over and over
out of ripe summer's bounty
to feed omnivorous appetites,
or listening to the scratch of prowlers
from the fragrant terraces, as they
dig-dig-dig, because they're mad
for bonemeal, uprooting plants and bulbs,
whole clumps, squirming and dank,
wherever they catch a whiff
of buried angel dust.

To be like Orpheus, who could talk
with animals in their own language:
in sleep I had that art, but now
I've waked into the separate
wilderness of age,
where the old, libidinous beasts
assume familiar shapes,
pretending to be tamed.

Raccoons! I can hear them
confabulating on the porch,
half-churring, half-growling,
bubbling to a manic hoot
that curdles the night-air.
Something out there appalls.
On the back door screen
a heavy furpiece hangs,
spreadeagled, breathing hard,
hooked by prehensile fingers,
with its pointed snout pressing in,
and the dark agates of its bandit eyes
furiously blazing. Behind,
where shadows deepen, burly forms
lumber from side to side
like diminished bears
in a flatfooted shuffle.
They watch me, unafraid.
I know they'll never leave,
they've come to take possession.

Provincetown 1984

The Old Darned Man

Back in the thirties, in the midst of the Great Depression, I fled the city and moved to a Connecticut farm. It was the period of my first marriage. We lived in an old gambrel house, built about 1740, on top of a ridge called Wormwood Hill. I had bought the house, together with more than 100 acres of woodland and pasture, for $500 down. It had no electricity, no heat, no running water, and it was in bad repair, but it was a great, beautiful house. I spent most of three years, working with my hands, making it habitable. At that time early American art and furniture were practically being given away. Poor as we were, we managed to fill the house with priceless stuff. We were so far from the city and from all signs of progress that we might as well have been living in another age.

One spring there appeared on the road, climbing up the hill, a man in a patchwork suit, with a battered silk hat on his head. His trousers and swallow-tailed coat had been mended so many times, with varicolored swatches, that when he approached us, over the brow of the hill, he looked like a crazyquilt on stilts.

He was an itinerant tinker, dried-out and old, thin as a scarecrow, with a high, cracked voice. He asked for pots and pans to repair, scissors and knives to sharpen. In the shade of the sugar maples, that a colonel in Washington's army was said to have planted, he set up his shop and silently went to work on the articles I handed to him.

When he was done, I offered him lunch in the kitchen. He would not sit down to eat, but accepted some food in a bag. I have been here before," he said to me quietly. On our way out, while we were standing in the front hall at the foot of the staircase, he suddenly cried, "I hear the worms tumbling in this house." "What do you mean?" I asked. He did not answer, but cupped his hands over his eyes. I took it as a bad omen, a fateful prophecy, about my house, my marriage. And so it turned out to be.

Some time later I learned that my visitor was a legendary figure, known throughout the countryside as the Old Darned Man. He had been a brilliant divinity student at Yale, engaged to a childhood sweetheart, with the wedding set for the day after graduation. But on that very day, while he waited at the church, the news was brought to him that she had run off with his dearest friend. Ever since then he had been wandering distractedly from village to village in his wedding clothes.

As for the worms, they belonged to a forgotten page in local history. Late in the nineteenth century the housewives of the region, dreaming of a fortune to be made, had started a cottage industry in silkworm culture, importing the worms from China. The parlors of every farmhouse were lined with stacks of silkworm trays, in which the worms munched on mulberry leaves, making clicking and whispering noises. That was the sound heard in my hall.

It's a story without a happy ending. The worms died; the dreams of riches faded; abandoned plows rusted in the farmyards; one breathless summer day a black-funneled twister wheeled up Wormwood Hill from the stricken valley, dismantling my house, my barn, my grove of sugar maples; the face of my bride darkened and broke into a wild laughter; I never saw the Old Darned Man again.

THE SCENE

—from Alexander Blok

Night. Street. Lamp. Drugstore.
A world of dim and sleazy light.
You may live twenty-five years more.
Nothing will change. No way out.

You die. You're born again and all
Will be repeated as before:
The cold ripple of a canal.
Night, Street. Lamp. Drugstore.

THE IMAGE-MAKER

A wind passed over my mind,
insidious and cold.
It is a thought, I thought,
but it was only its shadow.
Words came,
or the breath of my sisters,
with a black rustle of wings.
They came with a summons
that followed a blessing.
I could not believe
I too would be punished.
Perhaps it is time to go,
to slip alone, as at a birth,
out of this glowing house
where all my children danced.
Seductive Night! I have stood
at my casement the longest hour,
watching the acid wafer
of the moon slowly dissolving
in a scud of cloud, and heard
the farthest hidden stars
calling my name.
I listen, but I avert my ears
from Meister Eckhart's warning:
All things must be forsaken.
God scorns
to show Himself among images.

LAMPLIGHTER: 1914

What I remember most was not
the incident at Sarajevo,
but the first flying steamkettle
puffing round the bend,
churning up the dirt
between the rocky pastures
as it came riding high
on its red wheels
in a blare of shining brass;
and my bay stallion snorting,
rearing in fright, bolting,
leaving me sprawled on the ground;
and our buggy
careening out of sight,
those loose reins dangling,
racing toward its rendezvous
with Hammond's stone wall
in an explosion of wood and flesh,
the crack of smashed cannon bones.
Who are these strangers
sprung out of the fields?
It is my friend, almost my brother,
who points a gun
to the crooked head.

Once I was a lamplighter
on the Quinnapoxet roads,
making the rounds with Prince,
who was older than I and knew
by heart each of our stations,

needing no whoa of command
nor a tug at his bridle.
That was the summer I practiced
sleight-of-hand and fell asleep
over my picture-books of magic.
Toward dusk, at crossings
and at farmhouse gates,
under the solitary iron trees
I stood on the rim of the buggy wheel
and raised my enchanter's wand,
with its tip of orange flame,
to the gas mantles in their cages,
touching them, one by one,
till the whole countryside bloomed.

Day of Foreboding

Great events are about to happen.
I have seen migratory birds
in unprecedented numbers
descend on the coastal plain,
picking the margins clean.
My bones are a family in their tent
huddled over a small fire
waiting for the uncertain signal
to resume the long march.

Three Small Parables for My Poet Friends

1

Certain saurian species, notably the skink, are capable of shedding their tails in self-defense when threatened. The detached appendage diverts attention to itself by taking on a life of its own and thrashing furiously about. As soon as the stalking wildcat pounces on the wriggler, snatching it up from the sand to bite and maul it, the free lizard scampers off. A new tail begins to grow in place of the one that has been sacrificed.

2

The larva of the tortoise beetle has the neat habit of collecting its droppings and exfoliated skin into a little packet that it carries over its back when it is out in the open. If it were not for this fecal shield, it would lie naked before its enemies.

3

Among the Bedouins, the beggar poets of the desert are held in contempt because of their greed, their thievery and venality. Everyone in the scattered encampments knows that poems of praise can be bought, even by the worst of scoundrels, for food or money. Furthermore, these wandering minstrels are notorious for stealing the ideas, lines, and even whole songs of others. Often the recitation is interrupted by the shouts of the squatters around the campfire: "Thou liest. Thou stolest it from So-and-so!" When the poet tries to defend himself, calling for witnesses to vouch for his probity or, in extremity, appealing to Allah, his hearers hoot him down, crying, "Kassad, kaddab! A poet is a liar."

THE ROUND

Light splashed this morning
on the shell-pink anemones
swaying on their tall stems;
down blue-spiked veronica
light flowed in rivulets
over the humps of the honeybees;
this morning I saw light kiss
the silk of the roses
in their second flowering,
my late bloomers
flushed with their brandy.
A curious gladness shook me.

So I have shut the doors of my house,
so I have trudged downstairs to my cell,
so I am sitting in semi-dark
hunched over my desk
with nothing for a view
to tempt me
but a bloated compost heap,
steamy old stinkpile,
under my window;
and I pick my notebook up
and I start to read aloud
the still-wet words I scribbled
on the blotted page:
"Light splashed . . ."

I can scarcely wait till tomorrow
when a new life begins for me,
as it does each day,
as it does each day.

PASSING THROUGH

—on my seventy-ninth birthday

Nobody in the widow's household
ever celebrated anniversaries.
In the secrecy of my room
I would not admit I cared
that my friends were given parties.
Before I left town for school
my birthday went up in smoke
in a fire at City Hall that gutted
the Department of Vital Statistics.
If it weren't for a census report
of a five-year-old White Male
sharing my mother's address
at the Green Street tenement in Worcester
I'd have no documentary proof
that I exist. You are the first,
my dear, to bully me
into these festive occasions.

Sometimes, you say, I wear
an abstracted look that drives you
up the wall, as though it signified
distress or disaffection.
Don't take it so to heart.
Maybe I enjoy not-being as much
as being who I am. Maybe
it's time for me to practice
growing old. The way I look

at it, I'm passing through a phase:
gradually I'm changing to a word.
Whatever you choose to claim
of me is always yours;
nothing is truly mine
except my name. I only
borrowed this dust.

THE LONG BOAT

When his boat snapped loose
from its mooring, under
the screaking of the gulls,
he tried at first to wave
to his dear ones on shore,
but in the rolling fog
they had already lost their faces.
Too tired even to choose
between jumping and calling,
somehow he felt absolved and free
of his burdens, those mottoes
stamped on his name-tag:
conscience, ambition, and all
that caring.
He was content to lie down
with the family ghosts
in the slop of his cradle,
buffeted by the storm,
endlessly drifting.
Peace! Peace!
To be rocked by the Infinite!
As if it didn't matter
which way was home;
as if he didn't know
he loved the earth so much
he wanted to stay forever.

THE WELLFLEET WHALE

*A few summers ago, on Cape Cod, a whale foundered on the
beach, a sixty-three-foot finback whale. When the tide went
out, I approached him. He was lying there, in monstrous
desolation, making the most terrifying noises—rumbling—
groaning. I put my hands on his flanks and I could feel the
life inside him. And while I was standing there, suddenly he
opened his eye. It was a big, red, cold eye, and it was staring
directly at me. A shudder of recognition passed between us.
Then the eye closed forever. I've been thinking about whales
ever since.*

—Journal entry

I

You have your language too,
   an eerie medley of clicks
     and hoots and trills,
location-notes and love calls,
   whistles and grunts. Occasionally,
     it's like furniture being smashed,
or the creaking of a mossy door,
   sounds that all melt into a liquid
     song with endless variations,
as if to compensate
   for the vast loneliness of the sea.
     Sometimes a disembodied voice
breaks in as if from distant reefs,
   and it's as much as one can bear
     to listen to its long mournful cry,

a sorrow without name, both more
    and less than human. It drags
        across the ear like a record
running down.

    2
No wind. No waves. No clouds.
    Only the whisper of the tide,
        as it withdrew, stroking the shore,
a lazy drift of gulls overhead,
    and tiny points of light
        bubbling in the channel.
It was the tag-end of summer.
    From the harbor's mouth
        you coasted into sight,
flashing news of your advent,
    the crescent of your dorsal fin
        clipping the diamonded surface.
We cheered at the sign of your greatness
    when the black barrel of your head
        erupted, ramming the water,
and you flowered for us
    in the jet of your spouting.

    3
All afternoon you swam
    tirelessly round the bay,
        with such an easy motion,
the slightest downbeat of your tail,
    an almost imperceptible
        undulation of your flippers,

you seemed like something poured,
    not driven; you seemed
        to marry grace with power.
And when you bounded into air,
    slapping your flukes,
        we thrilled to look upon
pure energy incarnate
    as nobility of form.
        You seemed to ask of us
not sympathy, or love,
    or understanding,
        but awe and wonder.

That night we watched you
    swimming in the moon.
        Your back was molten silver.
We guessed your silent passage
    by the phosphorescence in your wake.
        At dawn we found you stranded on the rocks.

4

There came a boy and a man
    and yet other men running, and two
        schoolgirls in yellow halters
and a housewife bedecked
    with curlers, and whole families in beach
        buggies with assorted yelping dogs.
The tide was almost out.
    We could walk around you,
        as you heaved deeper into the shoal,
crushed by your own weight,
    collapsing into yourself,
        your flippers and your flukes
quivering, your blowhole

spasmodically bubbling, roaring.
    In the pit of your gaping mouth
you bared your fringework of baleen,
    a thicket of horned bristles.
    When the Curator of Mammals
arrived from Boston
    to take samples of your blood
    you were already oozing from below.
Somebody had carved his initials
    in your flank. Hunters of souvenirs
    had peeled off strips of your skin,
a membrane thin as paper.
    You were blistered and cracked by the sun.
    The gulls had been pecking at you.
The sound you made was a hoarse and fitful bleating.
What drew us, like a magnet, to your dying?
    You made a bond between us,
    the keepers of the nightfall watch,
who gathered in a ring around you,
    boozing in the bonfire light.
    Toward dawn we shared with you
your hour of desolation,
    the huge lingering passion
    of your unearthly outcry,
as you swung your blind head
    toward us and laboriously opened
    a bloodshot, glistening eye,
in which we swam with terror and recognition.

    5
Voyager, chief of the pelagic world,
    you brought with you the myth
    of another country, dimly remembered,

where flying reptiles
    lumbered over the steaming marshes
       and trumpeting thunder lizards
wallowed in the reeds.
    While empires rose and fell on land,
       your nation breasted the open main,
rocked in the consoling rhythm
    of the tides. Which ancestor first plunged
       head-down through zones of colored twilight
to scour the bottom of the dark?
    You ranged the North Atlantic track
       from Port-of-Spain to Baffin Bay,
edging between the ice-floes
    through the fat of summer,
       lob-tailing, breaching, sounding,
grazing in the pastures of the sea
    on krill-rich orange plankton
       crackling with life.
You prowled down the continental shelf,
    guided by the sun and stars
       and the taste of alluvial silt
on your way southward
    to the warm lagoons,
       the tropic of desire,
where the lovers lie belly to belly
    in the rub and nuzzle of their sporting;
       and you turned, like a god in exile,
out of your wide primeval element,
    delivered to the mercy of time.

    Master of the whale-roads,
let the white wings of the gulls
    spread out their cover.
       You have become like us,
disgraced and mortal.

PASSING THROUGH:
THE LATER POEMS

What makes the engine go?
Desire, desire, desire.
The longing for the dance
Stirs in the buried life.
One season only,
                    and it's done.

1995

MY MOTHER'S PEARS

Plump, green-gold, Worcester's pride,
  transported through autumn skies
    in a box marked HANDLE WITH CARE

sleep eighteen Bartlett pears,
  hand-picked and polished and packed
    for deposit at my door,

each in its crinkled nest
  with a stub of stem attached
    and a single bright leaf like a flag.

A smaller than usual crop,
  but still enough to share with me,
    as always at harvest time.

Those strangers are my friends
  whose kindness blesses the house
    my mother built at the edge of town

beyond the last trolley-stop
  when the century was young, and she
    proposed, for her children's sake,

to marry again, not knowing how soon
  the windows would grow dark
    and the velvet drapes come down.

Rubble accumulates in the yard,
  workmen are hammering on the roof,
    I am standing knee-deep in dirt

with a shovel in my hand.
       Mother has wrapped a kerchief round her head,
             her glasses glint in the sun.

When my sisters appear on the scene,
       gangly and softly tittering,
             she waves them back into the house

to fetch us pails of water,
       and they skip out of our sight
             in their matching middy blouses.

I summon up all my strength
       to set the pear tree in the ground,
             unwinding its burlap shroud.

It is taller than I. "Make room
       for the roots!" my mother cries,
             "Dig the hole deeper."

CHARIOT

In this image of my friend's studio,
where curiosity runs the shop, and you
can almost smell the nostalgic dust
settling on the junk of lost mythologies,
the artist himself stays out of view.
Yet anyone could guess
this is the magician's place
from his collection of conical hats
and the sprawled puppets on a shelf,
the broken as well as the whole,
that have grown to resemble him,
or the other way round.
Butterflies, gameboards, and bells,
strewn jacks and alphabet blocks,
spindles, old music scores—
the litter spreads from wall to wall.
If you could dig to the bottom,
you might expect to find
a child's plush heart,
a shining agate eye.
Here everything waits to be renewed.
That horse-age wagon wheel
propped in the corner
against an empty picture-frame,
even in its state of disrepair,
minus three spokes,
looks poised for flight.
Tomorrow, maybe, at the crack of a whip

a flock of glittering birds will perch
on its rim, a burnished stranger
wearing an enigmatic mask
will mount its hub
and the great battered wheel
will start to spin.

IN THE DARK HOUSE

"The injury cannot be healed; it extends through time,
and the Furies, in whose existence we are forced to believe
. . . perpetuate the tormentor's work by denying peace to
the tormented."

—Primo Levi

People had celebrated him as a god
because his art, they said, was magical,
sweeter to them than the soft spring rains
that blew off the lilac mountains,
secret as the wind whispering through the olives.
Eurydice, his lissome bride!
He made a caressing music
out of the vowels of her name.
All that he ever wanted was to sing of his love.

Where had they gone, that ragtag minstrel band,
those merry dancers, with whom he strolled
at the green earth's invitation,
their ranks swelling at each crossroad?
How young they were
who crowned him king of their carnival!
And the news raced ahead that at his passing
trees broke into blossom out of season,
nightingales and owls perched on his shoulders,
and down the winding country roads
processions of wild beasts,
great spotted cats, weasels, and wolves
tagged meekly at his heels, tamed by his song.

If he could reinvent those melting chords
struck from his nights of loneliness and need
that won reprieve in Hades' rancid halls,
would he rejoice again to see
the dark lord shed a cold, permissive tear?

He dared not look behind, nor could he guess
how distantly she trailed: that was the Law,
senseless and cruel, but still
the Law, imposing separate silences
on two who struggled up the fetid slope,
gasping for breath, through swirls of sulphur clouds
that parted to reveal, in oozing light,
covens of Harpies roosting on the walls,
and smoldering on the rock-strewn course ahead,
bonfires that seemed to plead with writhing arms.

At the blackened gate, a single step removed
from sunlight, birdcalls, and the heady air
he waited for her to join him
and to catch his hand, perhaps to murmur
the lost, impetuous, redemptive word.
Instead he heard her shrill, inhuman wail,
a tunnel-echo locked into his ears,
the cry of souls unsuited for this life,
having been touched by evil past forgiveness.

Yes, he had turned, as anybody would,
as certainly she knew he would, and saw her,
in that instant she was whisked away,
claw at the shawl that hid her from the world
to show him the ravaged face of all farewells
and the blank pennies of her defeated eyes.

As he sat in the dark, in the shuttered house,
Orpheus heard the women hooting in the street
outside, raving against him, blaming him
for their sister's loss. Apollo's priceless gift
lay dusty at his feet, so much a part of him
he wondered why its strings did not crack for grief.
How could he deny that frenzied mob,
not to be assuaged except by blood,
when his own heart cried worse?
He listened for the trampling on the stairs.

HALLEY'S COMET

Miss Murphy in first grade
wrote its name in chalk
across the board and told us
it was roaring down the stormtracks
of the Milky Way at frightful speed
and if it wandered off its course
and smashed into the earth
there'd be no school tomorrow.
A red-bearded preacher from the hills
with a wild look in his eyes
stood in the public square
at the playground's edge
proclaiming he was sent by God
to save every one of us,
even the little children.
"Repent, ye sinners!" he shouted,
waving his hand-lettered sign.
At supper I felt sad to think
that it was probably
the last meal I'd share
with my mother and my sisters;
but I felt excited too
and scarcely touched my plate.
So mother scolded me
and sent me early to my room.
The whole family's asleep
except for me. They never heard me steal
into the stairwell hall and climb
the ladder to the fresh night air.

Look for me, Father, on the roof
of the red brick building
at the foot of Green Street—
that's where we live, you know, on the top floor.
I'm the boy in the white flannel gown
sprawled on this coarse gravel bed
searching the starry sky,
waiting for the world to end.

HORNWORM: SUMMER REVERIE

Here in caterpillar country
I learned how to survive
by pretending to be a dragon.
See me put on that look
of slow and fierce surprise
when I lift my bulbous head
and glare at an intruder.
Nobody seems to guess
how gentle I really am,
content most of the time
simply to disappear
by melting into the scenery.
Smooth and fatty and long,
with seven white stripes
painted on either side
and a sharp little horn for a tail,
I lie stretched out on a leaf,
pale green on my bed of green,
munching, munching.

HORNWORM: AUTUMN LAMENTATION

Since that first morning when I crawled
into the world, a naked grubby thing,
and found the world unkind,
my dearest faith has been that this
is but a trial: I shall be changed.
In my imaginings I have already spent
my brooding winter underground,
unfolded silky powdered wings, and climbed
into the air, free as a puff of cloud
to sail over the steaming fields,
alighting anywhere I pleased,
thrusting into deep tubular flowers.

It is not so: there may be nectar
in those cups, but not for me.
All day, all night, I carry on my back
embedded in my flesh, two rows
of little white cocoons,
so neatly stacked
they look like eggs in a crate.
And I am eaten half away.

If I can gather strength enough
I'll try to burrow under a stone
and spin myself a purse
in which to sleep away the cold;
though when the sun kisses the earth
again, I know I won't be there.

Instead, out of my chrysalis
will break, like robbers from a tomb,
a swarm of parasitic flies,
leaving my wasted husk behind.

Sir, you with the red snippers
in your hand, hovering over me,
casting your shadow, I greet you,
whether you come as an angel of death
or of mercy. But tell me,
before you choose to slice me in two:
Who can understand the ways
of the Great Worm in the Sky?

THE SEA, THAT HAS NO ENDING . . .

"Green Sea *is one of a series of paintings {Philip}*
Guston did in 1976 *featuring a tangle of disembodied*
legs, bent at the knees and wearing flat, ungainly shoes,
grouped on the horizon of a deep green sea against a
salmon-colored backdrop . . . Its meaning eludes us."
      —descriptive note, Master Paintings in the Art
        Institute of Chicago

Who are we? Why are we here,
huddled on this desolate shore,
so curiously chopped and joined?—
broken totems, a scruffy tribe!
How many years have passed
since we owned keys to a door,
had friends, walked down familiar streets
and answered to a name? We try
not to remember the places
where we left pieces of ourselves
along the way, whether in ditches
at the side of foreign roads
or under signs that spell FOR HIRE
or naked between the sheets in cheap
motels. Does anybody care?
All the villagers have fled
from the sorry sight of us.
In the beginning we had faith
that the Master, who day and night
lets nothing escape the glare
from his invisible tower,

would soften at our appeals;
but we are baffled by his replies
even more than by his silences.
When we complain of the cruel sun
and the blisters popping in our skin
he turns our suffering against us:
A great wound, one you could claim
your very own, might have saved you.
Instead you let others do you in
with their small knives.
What is to become of us?
The sea, that has no ending,
is lapping at our feet.
How we long for the cleansing waters
to rise and cover us forever!
But he who reads our secret thoughts
rebukes us, saying: *You cannot hope*
to be restored unless you dare
to plunge head-down into the mystery
and there confront the beasts
that prowl on the ocean floor.
"Sacred monsters" is what he calls them.
If only we had strength enough
or nerve for a grand heroic action.
Habit has made it easier for us
to wait for the blessing of the tide.
It's really strange how much we miss
those people who came to gape and jeer;
we'd welcome their return, for company.
Why is the Master knocking at our ears,
demanding immediate attention?

In the acid of his voice we sense
the horns swelling at his temples
and little drops of spittle
bubbling at the corners of his mouth.
This is not an exhibition, he storms,
it's a life!

PROTEUS

At midday he rose on schedule from the flood
to stretch his limbs on the kelp-strewn shelf
of rock, where he could soak his bones
in the drippings of the sun
and watch, bemused, the monsters of the deep,
who were his sacred charge,
humping and snorting at their brutish games.

He was not envious of their rampant blood,
nor had he bargained for this keeper's role.
Their origins were buried in his past,
lost syllables in a language of forgetting.
Perhaps they were his misbegotten brood,
conceived by night in another age, but why
should he be vexed, as in his wanton prime,
by buzzing guilts and blames, that cloud of flies?
His burden was to see the future plain.

On shore, he knew, under the beetling crags
lurked bands of marauders in their painted skins,
waiting for him to lapse into a drowse,
when they would pounce upon him in repose
and pin him down, compelling him
to rip the sweating membrane from the void
and practice his excruciating art.

He was the world's supreme illusionist,
taught by necessity how to melt his cage,
slipping at will through his adversaries' grasp
by self-denial, displaying one by one

his famous repertoire of shifting forms,
from lion and serpent to fire and waterfall.
But now he was heavy in his heart, and languid,
sensing the time had come to leave his flock.
Must he prepare himself once more for the test?
He could not recollect the secret codes
that gave him access to his other lives.

Half-listening to the plashing of the oars,
a disembodied chorus from the sea,
he shut his dimming eyes
and did not stir. These were the dreaded boatmen
racing to his side, and these their hairy hands.
He heard barbaric voices crying, "Prophesy!"

Touch Me

Summer is late, my heart.
Words plucked out of the air
some forty years ago
when I was wild with love
and torn almost in two
scatter like leaves this night
of whistling wind and rain.
It is my heart that's late,
it is my song that's flown.
Outdoors all afternoon
under a gunmetal sky
staking my garden down,
I kneeled to the crickets trilling
underfoot as if about
to burst from their crusty shells;
and like a child again
marveled to hear so clear
and brave a music pour
from such a small machine.
What makes the engine go?
Desire, desire, desire.
The longing for the dance
stirs in the buried life.
One season only,
                    and it's done.
So let the battered old willow
thrash against the windowpanes
and the house timbers creak.
Darling, do you remember
the man you married? Touch me,
remind me who I am.

NOTES

INTELLECTUAL THINGS   1930

THE PIVOT. Original title, "Soul's Adventure."

HE. The narrative details are only loosely compatible with the Gospel texts. At a quasi-allegorical level, I tend to read this poem, written in my early twenties, as a projection of the mystery of the creative process.

NOCTURNE. Original title, "Death in Moonlight."

BETWEEN ME AND THE ROCK. Original title, "Me and the Rock."

THE LESSON. Excerpted from "For the Word Is Flesh," my first attempt to explore the theme of the lost father. As for the hypothetical "Florentine," he was undoubtedly suggested to me by an account I had recently read of the final hours of the author of *Remembrance of Things Past*. Marcel Proust was reported to have asked his servant to bring him a certain page wherein Bergotte is portrayed on his deathbed. "I have several retouchings to make here," Proust explained, "now that I find myself in the same predicament."

In Virgil's *Aeneid,* when Aeneas descends into Hades to visit his father, Anchises, he carries with him, on the advice of the Sibyl, a "golden bough" (presumably a sprig of mistletoe) as an amulet to assure his safe passage and return.

PASSPORT TO THE WAR   1944

REFLECTION BY A MAILBOX. Using dogs as experimental animals, Ivan Pavlov (1849–1936), Russian physiologist and psychologist, did important research in the physiology of the digestive glands and discovered the conditioned reflex. In 1904 he received the Nobel Prize in Physiology and Medicine.

THE LAST PICNIC. Written following the bombing of Pearl Harbor by the Japanese, December 7, 1941.

FATHER AND SON. The Gemara is the second and supplementary part of the Talmud, the oral law of the Jews, providing an extensive commentary by later rabbinical scholars on the traditional texts presented in the first part, the Mishna.

THE DAUGHTERS OF THE HORSELEECH. "The horseleach hath two daughters, crying, Give, give."—Proverbs 30:15.

THE RECKONING. Original title, "What Have You Done?"

THIS GARLAND, DANGER (IN SELECTED POEMS: 1928–1958)

THE APPROACH TO THEBES. As foretold by the oracle of Delphi, Oedipus is fated to kill his father Laius, King of Thebes, and marry Jocasta, his mother. Every effort by the principals to avert this catastrophe only makes it more inevitable.

My image of the Sphinx differs radically from the standard version, in which she is depicted as a homicidal creature with the head and breast of a woman and the body of a winged lion.

THE THIEF. "Mamertine blood" alludes to the Mamertine Prison in the Roman Forum, which has a dungeon reputed to have been occupied by St. Peter. The "baldpate [who] awaits his rhetorical cue" behind the balcony refers to Mussolini.

THE TESTING-TREE 1971

JOURNAL FOR MY DAUGHTER. Written during the period of student rebellion and mass demonstrations provoked by the Vietnam War. The "uncle-bear" in Part 5 is an evocation of Theodore Roethke on one of his visits in the early fifties.

AN OLD CRACKED TUNE. The first line is borrowed from an odious street song about a Jewish tailor that I recall from my student days in the twenties.

THE MAGIC CURTAIN. Frieda's song (literal translation):
    One, two, three, four, five, six, seven,
    what has become of my beloved?
    He is not here, he is not there.
    He's gone away to America.

AFTER THE LAST DYNASTY. Chairman Mao's summation of his strategy of guerrilla warfare: "Enemy advances, we retreat; enemy halts, we harass; enemy tires, we attack; enemy retreats, we pursue."

RIVER ROAD. Location: New Hope, Bucks County, Pennsylvania, where I lived for several years prior to my departure in 1941 for military service in World War II.

TRISTIA. Mandelstam's Latin title, signifying Poems of Sorrow, alludes to the elegiac epistles of Ovid, which the Roman poet began on his journey into exile in Tomis, a Black Sea outpost. Ovid spoke of the sorrow of exile, of his unconquerable will to survive and to write, of his loves, and of his hope that he might be allowed to return to Rome. Mandelstam (1891–1938) never returned from the prison camp to which Stalin sent him.

THE MOUND BUILDERS. The civilization of the Mound Builders, of whom regrettably little is known, flourished between A.D. 900 and 1100. The site of their community in Georgia was later held sacred by the Creek Nation. At the time of my visit to the Ocmulgee National Monument, in the spring of 1962, President Kennedy had just announced the resumption of nuclear testing by the United States.

THE GLADIATORS. The impulsive monk who tried to stop the bloodshed suffered his martyrdom at the hands of the enraged spectators about A.D. 400. The scandal of his dismemberment led to the proscription of man-to-man combats. In actual historical sequence, which I have telescoped, the barbarous Children's Crusades did not eventuate till the thirteenth century.

AROUND PASTOR BONHOEFFER. Dietrich Bonhoeffer was a German Lutheran pastor and theologian whose Christian conscience forced him, against the pacific temper of his spirit, to accept the necessity of political activism and to join in a conspiracy for the murder of Hitler. The plot failed, and he was arrested by the Gestapo (1943). On April 9, 1945, he was hanged at Flossenburg extermination camp. His brother Klaus and two brothers-in-law were also destroyed. Some of the details of the poem have their source in Bonhoeffer's two posthumous publications, *The Cost of Discipleship* and *Letters and Papers from Prison*, and in the biography by his disciple Eberhard Bethge.

BOLSHEVIKS. Aba Stolzenberg (1905–1941) was an obscure Yiddish poet who came to the United States from Poland. Irving Howe, in the course of compiling *A Treasury of Yiddish Poetry* (Holt, Rinehart and Winston, 1969) in collaboration with Eliezer Greenberg, introduced me to Stolzenberg's work and provided me with a transliteration of the text.

THE FLIGHT OF APOLLO. Written on the occasion of the flight of Apollo II and the first lunar landing, July 20, 1969.

KING OF THE RIVER. Within two weeks after leaving the ocean to swim up the rivers of the Northwest and spawn, the bounding Pacific salmon degenerates into an aged, colorless, and almost lifeless fish. The same geriatric process in humans takes some twenty to forty years.

CLEOPATRA, DANTE, BORIS PASTERNAK. Anna Akhmatova (1888–1966), friend and peer of Pasternak and Mandelstam, is one of the heroic figures of modern Russian poetry. During the Stalin Terror, her loved ones were killed or imprisoned and she herself was vilified, censored, and silenced. Like Dante in her poem, she refused to play the part of the humble penitent. In her tribute to Pasternak she plaits a garland for him out of favorite images from his work.

   The Daryal Gorge runs through the Caucasus into Georgia, which Pasternak often visited in the thirties to see his friends, the poets Paolo Yashvili and Titsian Tabidze, both of whom were to die in the purges.

   I am indebted to the late Max Hayward, fellow of St. Antony's College, Oxford, for his renderings of the Russian texts and his invaluable commentaries. Our close collaboration for several years led to the publication in 1973 of *Poems of Akhmatova* (Atlantic-Little, Brown), subsequently reissued in paperback by Houghton Mifflin.

THE ARTIST. Written following the suicide in New York of my friend the painter Mark Rothko, on February 25, 1970.

THE TESTING-TREE. When I was a boy in Worcester, Massachusetts, my family lived on top of a hill, at the thin edge of the city, with the woods beyond. Much of the time I was alone, but I learned how not to be lonely, exploring the surrounding fields and the old Indian trails. In the games that I improvised, most of them involved with running, climbing, and a variety of ball-skills, I was a fierce competitor, representing in turn myself and my imaginary opponent. It did not occur to me to be surprised that "I" was always the winner.

The stone-throwing that figures in the poem was of a somewhat special order, since it did more than try my skill: it challenged destiny. My life hinged on the three throws permitted me, according to my rules. If I hit the target-oak once, somebody would love me; if I hit it twice, I should be a poet; if I scored all three times, I should never die. A friend of mine tells me that what I have recorded here is recognizable as an ancient ritual, and that the patriarchal scarred oak, as I have described it, is transparently a manifestation of the King of the Wood. Such mysteries for a Worcester childhood!

THE LAYERS (IN *THE POEMS OF STANLEY KUNITZ 1928–1978*)

WHAT OF THE NIGHT? Several of the details in Part 2 derive from Franz Kafka's story "The Country Doctor."

QUINNAPOXET. Quinnapoxet was a backwater village, no longer in existence, outside Worcester, Massachusetts, where I spent many of my childhood summers as a boarder on the Buteau family farm. The poem came to me in a dream.

WORDS FOR THE UNKNOWN MAKERS. Rose Slivka, then editor of the periodical *Craft Horizons*, gave me *carte blanche* to write on the unprecedented exhibition "The Flowering of American Folk Art 1776–

1876," at the Whitney Museum of American Art, New York, February 1 to March 24, 1974. This suite of poems, with photographic illustrations from the exhibition, appeared in the February 1974 issue of *Craft Horizons*.

To a Slave Named Job. "Job's Cigar Store Indian," in polychromed wood, is believed to have been made by a slave (c. 1825) for a tobacconist in Freehold, New Jersey.

Sacred to the Memory. Based on an unsigned watercolor, "Mourning Picture for Polly Botsford and Her Children," painted c. 1813 and found in Connecticut.

Trompe l'Oeil. Several nineteenth-century country artisans became masters of illusion, developing techniques that enabled them to simulate, on ordinary pine, the inlays, veneers, and graining of expensive furniture.

A Blessing of Women. Jean Lipman and Alice Winchester, who organized the Whitney exhibition and made a book out of it, provided the biographical information incorporated into this poem. See *The Flowering of American Folk Art*, 1776–1876 (Viking Press, 1974).

THE CRYSTAL CAGE. Contributed, together with my illustrative collage, to Dore Ashton's *A Joseph Cornell Album* (Viking Press, 1974). My title is taken from one of Cornell's early boxes.

SIGNS AND PORTENTS. Since this poem was written in 1976–1977, Ramses II has been returned to Egypt from Paris after treatment for his infection; the delicate operation of removing the Caryatids from the Erectheum has been completed; the Caves of Lascaux are open again to visitors, but on a limited basis; no further word has reached me from Saint Helena about the fate of Jonathan the giant tortoise.

FIRESTICKS. For José Guerrero (1914–1991). Originally published in a portfolio with related serigraphs by the Spanish-born painter: *Fos-*

forencias, by José Guerrero (Galeria Juana Mordo, Madrid, and El Museo de Arte Abstracto Español, Cuenca, 1971).

THE LINCOLN RELICS. The exhibition of Lincoln relics was held at the Library of Congress during the term of my appointment as Consultant in Poetry, 1974–1976. My previous experience of living in Washington had been during World War II, when I was in military service (alluded to in Part 4). The apostrophe ("Mr. President . . .") at the close of Part 3 refers to the Watergate hearings and the subsequent resignation of President Nixon in 1974. In 1980, during the Carter administration, I was given the opportunity to read this poem at the White House.

MEDITATIONS ON DEATH, "La Morte Meditata." My original version of Ungaretti's hermetic poem, titled "Death Thoughts," was written during his triumphal visit to the United States in the spring of 1970. By invitation of the Academy of American Poets, Ungaretti's American translators participated in his reading at the Guggenheim Museum in New York. Ungaretti (1888–1970) died shortly after his return to Italy.

NEXT-TO-LAST THINGS 1985

THE ABDUCTION. Elements of memory, dream, and fantasy entered into the making of this poem, which was triggered by my reading of *Missing Time*, a work on UFO abductions, by Budd Hopkins (Richard Marek, 1981). See "The Layers: Some Notes on 'The Abduction,'" in *Next-to-Last Things: New Poems and Essays* (Atlantic Monthly Press, 1985).

THE SCENE. Alexander Blok (1880–1921), the most famous of the Russian Symbolist poets, died in poverty and despair.

THE IMAGE-MAKER. In the teachings of Meister Eckhart (c. 1260–1327), German mystic and theologian, God is the only true reality and the human soul is the only place in the universe where God can reveal Himself in the truth of His being.

THREE SMALL PARABLES FOR MY POET FRIENDS. My information about the Bedouin beggar poets has its source in *The Manners and Customs of the Rwala Bedouins*, by Alois Musil (American Geographical Society, 1928).

THE WELLFLEET WHALE. Written in 1981 and first read at Harvard that year as the Phi Beta Kappa poem. The actual beaching of the whale, in Wellfleet Harbor, occurred on September 12, 1966.

PASSING THROUGH: THE LATER POEMS 1995

MY MOTHER'S PEARS. For Carol and Greg Stockmal, of Worcester, Massachusetts, whose annual gift of "my mother's pears" inspired this poem.

CHARIOT. For Varujan Boghosian. Written for the retrospective exhibition of his work at the Hood Museum of Art, Dartmouth College, March 25–June 25, 1989.

IN THE DARK HOUSE. The epigraph is from Primo Levi's last work *The Drowned and the Saved* (Summit Books, 1988). More than forty-two years after his release from Auschwitz, Levi (1919–1987) jumped to his death in Turin, Italy, down the main stairwell of the apartment building in which he had been born.

In the standard version of the myth of Orpheus and Eurydice, from which I depart in some details, as Orpheus approaches the exit from the underworld he succumbs to the temptation to look behind him to see if his bride is following. As a consequence of his impulsive behavior, Eurydice is dragged back into Hades, doomed to languish there forever. In the land of the living, grief-stricken Orpheus is eventually torn into pieces by the Maenads, female attendants of Dionysus. Flung into the Hebrus, his head and his lyre float downriver to the sea, the head still crying out the name of his beloved and the lyre, "Apollo's priceless gift," still playing.

HORNWORM: SUMMER REVERIE, HORNWORM: AUTUMN LAMENTATION. The familiar tomato hornworm, dreaded because of its voracious appetite, is the larval stage of the beautiful and speedy hawkmoth, or sphinx moth, so called from the caterpillar's habit, when disturbed, of elevating the front part of its body and drawing back its head. Some observers find this posture more suggestive of a threatening cobra than of the enigmatic Sphinx of ancient Egypt and Greece. Hornworms are frequently parasitized by braconids, little ichneumon flies that inject eggs beneath their skin. The emerging larvae feed internally on the soft caterpillar tissues until they are mature enough to bore their way to the surface and form cocoons. By this time, death is near for the defenseless host.

THE SEA, THAT HAS NO ENDING . . . Philip Guston (1913–1980) was one of the major American painters of his generation. My poem incorporates memories of him and of our conversations.

PROTEUS. "In the myth of Proteus we are told that at midday he rose from the flood and slept in the shadow of the rocks of the coast. Around him lay the monsters of the deep, whom he was charged with tending. He was famous for his gift of prophecy, but it was a painful art, which he was reluctant to employ. The only way anyone could compel him to foretell the future was by pouncing on him while he slept in the open. It was in order to escape the necessity of prophesying that he changed his shape . . . If he saw that his struggles were useless, he resumed his

ordinary appearance, spoke the truth, and plunged back into the sea."
—From "Poet of Transformations," in the collection of my essays, *A Kind of Order, A Kind of Folly* (Atlantic-Little, Brown, 1975); originally published in *The New Republic,* January 23, 1965.

TOUCH ME. The opening line is recalled from "As Flowers Are," in my *Selected Poems 1928–1958* (Atlantic-Little, Brown, 1958), p. 92 in this collection.

Acknowledgments

My thanks to the publications in which, through the years, my poems have first appeared.

INTELLECTUAL THINGS: *The Commonweal, The Dial, Herald-Tribune Books, Hound and Horn, The Nation, The New American Caravan, The New Republic,* and *Poetry*

PASSPORT TO THE WAR: *The American Mercury, The Commonweal, The Dial, Direction, Hound and Horn, The Nation, The New American Caravan, The New Republic,* and *The Saturday Review of Literature*

SELECTED POEMS: 1928–1958: *The Avon Book of Modern Writing, Botteghe Oscure, The Hudson Review, The Nation, The New Republic, New World Writing, The New York Quarterly, Partisan Review, Poetry,* and *The Saturday Review of Literature*

THE TESTING-TREE: *Art in America, The Atlantic Monthly, Book Week, The New American Review, The New Leader, The New York Quarterly, The New York Review of Books, The New York Times,* and *The Times Literary Supplement* [London]

THE POEMS OF STANLEY KUNITZ 1928–1978: *The American Poetry Review, Antaeus, The Atlantic Monthly, Craft Horizons, Iowa Review, Malahat Review, The Nation, The New England Review,* and *The New Yorker*

NEXT-TO-LAST THINGS: *The American Poetry Review, Antaeus, The Atlantic Monthly, The New Yorker,* and *Salmagundi*

PASSING THROUGH: *The American Poetry Review, The Atlantic Monthly, The Gettysburg Review, The New Yorker,* and *Poetry Ireland Review*

Index of Titles and First Lines